ND PRINCIPLES IN FLORAL DESIGN

II. CONSTRUCTING THE DESIGN

Organizing the elements while controlling the **inherent relationships:**

Repetition
Variation
Contrast
Proportion
Direction

subject to the
co-ordinating principles:

Dominance
Balance
Rhythm

to achieve
attributes of aesthetic design:

Harmony
Distinction
Expression (optional)
Beauty

To Jerry Knoth
who shares my trials and
joys of Flower Arranging

Anne B Smith

Sept 81

New Approach

to Design Principles

A Comprehensive Analysis

of Design Elements and Principles

in Floral Design

Anne Bernat Sutter

Flower Arrangements by the Author

ISBN 0-9600120-3-6

Printed in United States of America

Anne Bernat Sutter
Fourth Edition, 1978

SUTTER PUBLISHING CO.   •   CREVE COEUR, MO.

To my

HUSBAND

in appreciation of his

patience and understanding

INTRODUCTION

Learning to arrange flowers is like learning a new language. Just as you can learn to speak a language by listening, observing, and repeating what you have heard, without ever seeing the inside of a grammar or dictionary, so the interested student of arranging can become adept at arranging by observing the work of others at flower shows, demonstrations, and lectures.

But no one could become a profound linguist or writer without some knowledge of grammar or sentence structure, so the serious student of arranging and the flower show judge must be able to analyze and understand the complex relationship of design elements and principles as applied to the art of arranging with plant material.

Since the first requisite for the flower arranging judge is, that she be an arranger, and since the arranger, in competition, hopes to induce favorable reaction of the judge, the problems they face and their solutions are mutual.

The following text has been written with these mutual problems in mind. May it serve to:

1. Analyze plant material, within its physical limitations, in terms of its visual forces.

2. Guide the power of perception to verify the universal nature of design principles.

3. Coordinate the visual forces, without regard to previous association or traditional usage, but by means of design principles, to satisfy the aesthetic sense.

ACKNOWLEDGMENTS

To my many friends who have encouraged me during the preparation of this book, I am deeply grateful. In particular, I want to express my appreciation to Mrs. Arthur Mueller and Prof. James E. Smith, Jr., for their critical evaluation of the text; and to thank Mrs. Willis Marshall and my daughter-in-law Margaret Sutter for their valued assistance.

Photographs by Earl Webb Studio, *except*

Francis Scheidegger, *pp.* 10, 11, 20, 60, 61, 90, 97, 102, **126, 143, 150, 154.**

Wm. Kleefisch, *pp.* 76, 113

Jackson & Perkins, *p.* 74

The author, *p.* 153, back cover

CONTENTS

CONTENTS

PART ONE

COMPONENTS

FROM GARDENING

THE MEDIUM

OTHER COMPONENTS

From Gardening---
To Floral Design

FROM GARDENING

It all started with the automobile. The automobile created a new freedom of living, unfettered by the need to be within walking distance of daily essentials or by dependency on public transportation. The grand exodus from cities to suburban homesites began. An interest in lawns, shrubs, and flowers followed. The homemaker turned to the garden club for answers. There followed the sudden growth of the garden club movement — its primary purpose being to advance gardening in all its aspects.

As Summer follows Spring, after the planting came the flowers. Next came the flower show and its stimulating competition. Competition spurred a surge of further interest in everything, horticultural and artistic, that might help attain the coveted blue ribbon. Flower arranging became a fascinating challenge.

Gardening is America's foremost hobby. To many it has become a way of life. Gardens and flowers are an integral part of the American home. The love of flowers has been the leavening agent that has made flower arranging a continuous challenge to gardeners and homemakers. Horticulture is the "bread and meat" of gardening; flower arranging, the "dessert."

It is said that a living art is modified by and reflects the spirit of the times. Although we are living in a "space" age, gardeners are particularly earthbound. Flower arranging thus reflects our interest in gardening.

TO FLORAL DESIGN

Flower Arranging is the art of organizing design elements, inherent in cut plant material, and such other components as may be related thereto, with intent to induce an aesthetic appeal.

Although the term "flower arrangement" might appear restricted to flowers, while "floral design" and "design with plant material," would include all plant forms, and the simple term "arrangement" might apply to other mediums, thru long usage, all have been accepted as having similar meanings. In this text these terms will be used interchangeably.

THE PURPOSE

Why arrange flowers? People enjoy flowers! In arranging flowers we make it possible for flowers to give even greater enjoyment.

THE SCOPE

Every piece of plant material *is* organized form and color having more or less aesthetic qualities. However, in a bunch of flowers, or in any random grouping of flowers, design relationship is apt to be poor.

A flower arrangement starts with plant material having intrinsic form and color and aesthetic qualities, and without changing its essential character, further relates plant material to each other, to the container, and to the space it occupies.

3

In the spectrum of the visual arts, we find representational painting and sculpture on the one end, then subjective abstract, then flower arranging, with non-representational abstract on the other end.

The medium of plant material is adaptable to some extent to subjective abstract in the one direction from conventional flower arranging, and to non-representational abstract in the other.

Beyond the scope of flower arranging are other fields which touch it in some areas.

The pineapple-turkey, the radish-rose, and junior's carrot-man are made of plant material, but are properly in the field of representational crafts. The polished wooden base has become a manufactured item.

When plant material has been so completely altered, distorted, mutilated or used in an unnatural manner, so that it has lost its essential character, the resulting design may be abstract art, but is no longer floral design.

Assemblages, mobiles, and other abstract designs consisting of plastic, metal, etc., but devoid of plant material, are in another field of art.

FLORAL DESIGN AN ART FORM

Flower arranging in America is a young art. Its age can be reckoned in decades, and during this time it has existed in the shadow of the classical arts, particularly painting and sculpture. It has emerged, from what some felt was a passing fancy, to an art form in its own right. It is now taking its rightful place in American culture. It has its own medium—living plant material—a medium unlike that of the traditional arts.

A DIFFERENT MEDIUM

How does the medium of floral design differ from that of the painter or sculptor?

The painter creates two-dimensional forms, from a medium that is *form-less*, and creates his color by mixing. The sculptor creates his three-dimensional forms, also from a form-less medium, with little concern about color. Both create their design elements and apply design principles to them at the *same time*.

We *grow* our medium — living plant material — a medium in which design elements are inherent and which nature has already organized, more or less, according to design principles. From this preorganized material we *select* or *reject* according to the elements and principles inherent in it. We do change its form—automatically as it is cut from the plant; and we can and do modify it further, primarily by cutting away. We can do little to improve its color, so prefer its color as nature provided. We then reorganize this preorganized material into our ultimate design.

Design elements and principles are the same for all fields of art, but since the medium used in each varies, the problems involved in each art are different.

So that Flower Arranging need no longer exist in the shadow of the other arts, but assume its rightful importance in American culture, it is necessary that we analyze design elements and principles IN THE LIGHT OF THESE DIFFERENCES.

In the following chapters, we present the components of a flower arrangement.

In Part Two we analyze the elements inherent in plant material, the forces they exert, and their forces in design.

In Part Three we describe the relationships existing in every grouping of plant material, which must be controlled.

In Part Four we explain the relationships that may be created.

In Part Five we conclude with the objectives of design.

The Medium

Cut plant material essentially unchanged in character is the medium in the art of flower arranging. This includes any part of a plant, such as flowers, buds, leaves, stems, fruit, seeds, etc. In this text the use of fresh plant material is implied, unless otherwise stated.

Every art medium has its own charactertistics and limitation which are inherited by the ultimate design. These the artist must recognize, respect, and control.

Plant material is living, growing, and perishable. It is predetermined in form and color and is preorganized. The arranger's supply thereof is unpredictable and uncontrollable.

The paint in a modern abstract painting or the clay or plastic in a modern piece of sculpture is not subject to any of these limitations of plant material.

A LIVING, GROWING MEDIUM

In order to be functional in design, plant material must have physical and structural strength. Fresh, turgid plant material possesses structural strength, as opposed to wilted material, which does not.

Plant material normally receives its supply of moisture from its root system, and when cut, from its lower stem end. Consequently, all plant material that requires water to remain turgid and living must have a stem in water.

Most of the form and color for a flower arrangement is found in the terminal portion of plant material. These are thus on the opposite end of the stem that must be in water. This stem must therefore be long enough to reach from the position of the element in the design to the water. The placement of elements in other arts has no such physical restrictions.

Foliage that remains turgid for several days, although out of water, and flowers that remain turgid for the greater part of their life expectancy, although out of water, can be used with greater leeway in design. Among these are cactus and other succulents, mature evergeen foliage, and some gardenias, hibiscus, hemerocallis, and iris.

Most plant material continues to grow as long as it is kept alive; therefore it is a constantly changing medium. Within a few hours or overnight, the rosebud will open to a full-blown rose, or the full-blown rose will change to another color; the tip of the snapdragon will turn upward; the tulip stem will straighten and be an inch longer; the wisteria vine will reach for a support. A design created today will be different tomorrow.

A PERISHABLE MEDIUM

Plant material is perishable while growing, but this is accelerated after being cut. Aside from a general knowledge of proper preparation and conditioning of material, we must be familiar with the particular material we are using.

Generally, flowers have a shorter life expectancy than foliage, stems, seedpods, etc. Flowers that unfold, such as the morning glory, moonvine, or four-o'clock, may have but a few hours of life, so may be unsuitable as cut flowers. Most hibiscus and hemerocallis fold their petals at sundown, so are suitable for daytime arrangements only. Flowers such as the zinnia, dahlia, chrysanthemums, and others that take several days to grow from bud to flower also take longer before they perish. Pollinated flowers die sooner than unpollinated flowers or double ones where the reproductive organs are vestigial. Spike flowers may last longest, but this is only because new florets, higher or lower on the stem, are opening while the older florets are closing.

The more mature foliage is, the longer it will live after being cut. Thus broadleaf evergreen is the longest lasting foliage for it. has grown for more than one temperate season. On the other hand, tender young tips that have not yet developed a strong cellular structure may wilt immediately beyond recovery.

PREDETERMINED AND PREORGANIZED FORM AND COLOR

Design elements are inherent in plant material. The form and color of every flower, leaf, or stem is determined before we cut it or otherwise acquire it. In addition nature has already applied design principles to these inherent elements.

The following qualities as listed in various scales of points for judging horticultural specimens illustrate the inherent nature of design in plant material: Color, form, size, texture, substance; branching, pattern, distinction. The first group of qualities are the design elements found in plant material. The second group, refers to the manner in which elements are already organized. In fact, plant material may sometimes be used "as is," without further organizing.

The fact that plant material is already organized into a design spells the great difference between painting or sculpture and flower arranging. It is because some of our objectives are already partly achieved that flower arranging is of interest to the average homemaker or gardener who has no inclination for the other arts.

The arranger's problem is one of selecting or rejecting preorganized form and color and reorganizing that which serves her purpose.

Practice in selection of form and color in plant material automatically trains the eye in rejection of material. Elimination or rejection is often the beginner's biggest headache. Having brought together a supply of material after considerable effort, she finds that she must reject with a firm hand. It may have the form or color she requires, but may not be organized in the desired pattern; or it may have the desired pattern but the wrong form or color for her purpose.

UNPREDICTABLE AND UNCONTROLLABLE SUPPLY

Getting the necessary supply of plant material for one arrangement for a flower show can be a project in itself. It involves growing and cultivating quantities and kinds of flowers and foliage that may at some time be useful. It means getting from neighbors, garden club members and other friends. It means making the rounds of local florists, and it often includes scouring the countryside for native plant material, including brush and weeds. All of these possible sources of supply are limited by the season of bloom; by frost, rain, drought, and heat; and by what was planted by us, our friends, or the commercial grower, this year, last year, or ten years ago.

The artist can "create" the blossoms of a tulip tree or the opening buds of a flowering horsechestnut in a short time. We must first buy a tree, plant it, and then wait six to ten years before our medium is available. Even then it is available for perhaps ten days out of the year. We could hardly combine the horsechestnut buds with bronze dahlias, even though both are related in size, color, and texture, because one is available only in the Spring, the other in the Fall.

OF INFINITE VARIETY

There is infinite variety of size, form, color and texture in plant material. In fact, no two flowers, leaves, fruits, or stems, nor their spacing, are ever exactly alike. Thus the arranger can never make exactly the same design a second time. Because of this each flower arrangement presents a new challenge.

The brief life expectancy of flowers and the fact that they can be arranged only when they are available in the garden, at the florist, or from the woods or fields, has turned some arrangers to the use of less flowers and more of other material — sometimes even artificial flowers and foliage—as her medium. But it is only the arranger who has no interest in growing flowers who willingly relegates plant material to such a minimum role. The arranger who grows her own flowers, foliage, shrubs, and vines accepts and respects the charactertistics and limitations of her plant material.

The medium of plant material is living, growing, perishable, of predetermined and preorganized form and color, in unpredictable and uncontrollable supply, and of infinite variety, but therein lies its never-ending challenge.

Other Components

THE CONTAINER

The container is the receptacle which holds the plant material, water, and some or all mechanics. It includes bases or stands, or may be one of the these alone.

Plant material, being a physical component, must be supported on something. A base or stand may perform this function. However, most plant material requires water to remain in a turgid or living condition and since water must be contained from all directions except the top, the water-holding container *under* the plant material becomes an essential part of the arrangement.

Exceptions are corsages and mobiles which are not supported on a horizontal surface.

The container itself may be of two parts: one visible, which becomes a part of the design; the other one, "behind the scenes," which actually holds the plant material, water or mechanics.

In the design on page 167 a container between the two pieces of driftwood, actually holds the plant material.

Since the container is visible at the same time as the plant material — although its purpose is purely functional — it becomes a part of the design. Design elements inherent in it must be reckoned with the same as those in the plant material itself.

MECHANICS

Mechanics are those contrivances used to control the direction of the plant material.

In organizing plant material into a design the direction of the plant material from the point of support and at other points in the design must be controlled by suitable mechanics.

Mechanics that are large and strong enough to control the direction of plant material seldom add to the attractiveness of the design. Therefore it is best that they be concealed inside of an opaque container, or in back of, or between other plant material.

Often containers adequate in other respects do not conceal the mechanics therein, or other mechanics cannot be hidden. Since any visible portion becomes a part of the visual design, the arranger must decide whether the visible mechanics or the attempt to conceal them are more detractive. If mechanics cannot be concealed effectively, and they detract from the ultimate design, they should be obscure rather than obvious.

Since it is preferable that mechanics be concealed, they are not included in the further study of design analysis.

The background is a component part of every design. It includes everything in the areas in back of, underneath, above, and on either side of the arrangement, within a visual frame, a frame of reference, or a physical frame. In the design on page 156 the color of the wallpaper and the pattern on it become part of the design.

VISUAL FRAME

The background within the visual frame includes everything that the viewer sees while looking at an arrangement. Our eyes function so that as we look at anything we see all that immediately surrounds it. We cannot visually isolate an arrangement, thereby seeing only the plant material and container without seeing all that the eye encompasses at the same time. If the arrangement is not in the center of our visual frame, we can and do change the visual frame by turning our heads or changing our position in order to get a better viewing angle, or "to get a better look at it."

THE FREE STANDING ARRANGEMENT

The free standing arrangement or the arrangement to integrate with space may be viewed from all sides. It has no background *immediately* behind it. Instead it is viewed against a more distant background. Its background may be the windows, walls, and furniture on the opposite side of the living or dining room; or the people moving about in the next aisle and the flower arrangements on the next table, in the flower show. It is also a variable background — one that changes constantly as the position and consequently the visual frame of the viewer changes.

FRAME OF REFERENCE

In the home the background is usually determined by a frame of reference. The frame of reference is the border established by the surrounding objects. The buffet arrangement is related to the buffet, and the objects on the buffet, on the side or above it, all enclosing directly or indirectly the wall space behind the arrangement. The mantel arrangement is related to the fireplace, the mantel, the wallpaper, and nearby objects, etc. A flower show class that calls for "an arrangement suitable for, etc." implies a frame of reference.

For an arrangement viewed at eye level or one predominantly vertical, the area in back of it becomes the center of the background area. For a horizontal arrangement or one viewed from above, the surface beneath is the most important one.

An arrangement in the center of the dining room table is in both of these categories. It may first be seen against a lace cloth and wood grain of the table top, in the frame of reference which includes the table appointments. Later, after the guests are seated, other guests become part of the visual frame. The patio table arrangement that starts with a red checkered cloth and heavy pottery dishes as the background, may change to the brick backside of your neighbor's garage for some of your guests, and a scarlet maple several doors away, for others.

PHYSICAL FRAME

Since the visual frame is so all-inclusive, the artist frames his picture with a white border, or a wooden frame, or both—physical means of containing the eye and the interest of the viewer within specific limits and to keep nearby and extraneous material out.

The flower show background shuts out all things beyond and keeps them out of the picture. Frames or dividers help to stop the eye and thereby contain the eye and interest within a predetermined area. The flower show niche is a three-dimensional enclosure which employs both of these devices. The physical frame serves to define the background which the arranger wants the arrangement to be related to, and to exclude what she does not want.

It is never a question whether to have a background or not—since a background is always present —but whether the background enhances or detracts as in the pictures on pages 10 and 11; and if it detracts, whether it can or should be changed.

When flowers are plentiful in the garden, how often have we made an arrangement, then carried it from one place in the house to another, to find the "right" spot for it—thereby conceding that the background is always a part of the picture.

However, the physical frame or border, the flower show niche, or the frame of reference, and such material as they already enclose should not be as important as the arrangement itself. But since the background is usually *fixed* or *predetermined*—in the flower show, by the staging committee; in the home, by the walls and furnishings—it becomes the component which we must consider first.

We start with the frame and relate the arrangement to it. Only the photographer can do otherwise. He may start with the arrangement and relate the frame to it. He may do this while composing the arrangement in the camera, or by cropping after the picture is developed. While composing he may even put an over-size arrangement or a miniature in the same frame.

The army wants its men and equipment to move unnoticed from place to place. It cannot change the background, so its camouflage department creates designs that are lost against it. In a flower show, we too, often have no control over the background furnished by the committee. However, we want to stimulate attention (especially that of the judges) so our problem is to create designs which project from the background the committee may have supplied.

The background—whether it be a painted wall or a patterned drapery in the living room, a piece of plywood in the flower show, or a planting of shrubs along the patio—**is the canvas on which the design is executed.**

OPTIONAL COMPONENTS

Components in a flower arrangement, other than the plant material, container, and background, are optional.

Flowers are congenial with many natural forms, such as rocks, sea shells and weathered wood, and with man-made objects, such as figurines and candles. If used, a natural form or man-made object should be incorporated into—not added to—a design of plant material. It may be used solely for its contribution of

form or color, or it may be used to assist in conveying the arranger's intent in an expressive or interpretive design. It may be an accessory, which is subordinate in the design, or it may be a feature, in which case the plant material is of subordinate interest, as in the design on page 12.

If an optional component is used, its design elements must be considered in the same manner as those of other components.

The Background. It is never a question of having a background or not—the background is always an integral part of the design. It may detract from the design as on the left, or serve to enhance as above.

Optional Components. Figure used as a feature. The plant material, although of greater amount, is of subordinate interest.

PART TWO

DESIGN ELEMENTS

STRUCTURAL and CHROMATIC DESIGN

LINE and FORM

SPACE

SIZE

COLOR FACTORS

CHROMATIC ELEMENTS

TEXTURE

PATTERN

Structural and Chromatic Design

The first step in creating design is selection of elements. What may appear to be selection of components is in fact selection of elements. It involves evaluating separate and preorganized components in terms of design elements.

Design elements are the basic visual attributes of which a design is composed. They are the visual qualities of physical material. Each design element exerts a visual force to which the eye and mind react.

It is our *response* to these forces exerted by the design elements, inherent in plant material, that determines how we shall use them in our design. Thus each element performs a *function* in design.

"DOUBLE EXPOSURE"

Every design of plant material is composed of two designs, one superimposed on the other:

1. **The structural design.**

2. **The chromatic design.**

The structural design is the basic one. It is composed of form and its related elements.

The chromatic design is superimposed on the structural design. It is composed of color and its related elements.

Color in plant material never exists per se. It is always superimposed on form. In a similar manner chromatic design is always superimposed on structural design. The opposite could not be true. The arranger cannot begin with a color design and superimpose the structural design on it, such as the abstract painter can.

THE STRUCTURAL ELEMENTS

The structural elements are:

1. Line—linear form.

2. Form—shapes, open, and closed forms.

3. Space—created by line and form.

4. Size—modifies form.

The structural elements are both tangible and visual.

THE CHROMATIC ELEMENTS

The chromatic elements are:

1. Hue—the name of a color.

2. Value—variations of a hue.

3. Texture—modifies color.

Hue and value are purely visual. Texture is tangible and visual. It modifies both form and color, but its greatest impact is on color, so is included in the chromatic elements.

By means of a black and white photograph we can *partially* separate these two designs for purpose of analysis. Here the structural elements remain, but of the chromatic elements, hues and all values of hues are eliminated, leaving only values of gray and texture.

A comparison of a black and white photograph and the actual arrangement it depicts or a color photograph thereof as on pages 16 and 17 helps us to study the visual impact of each separately.

The Structural Design. The black and white photograph records only the structural design. Here the strength or weakness of line, form, and space can be analyzed without the influence of color.

The Chromatic Design. The color photograph records the whole arrangement — the structural design and the color design. An analysis of both photographs helps us to determine the separate impact of each. (Container by Mrs. C. W. Thomas.)

A Single Structural Design May Have Many Chromatic Designs. Here the two structural designs are essentially the same; however, each has a distinctly different chromatic design.

Related Color Harmony. Since this depends on variation of hue and value, rather than contrast, it would make a poor black and white print.

The black and white photograph records the structural design by means of color value. The sharpness of a black and white photograph depends on *contrast* of color value since it distinguishes an individual element or component from another, and the whole structural silhouette from its background.

A *related* color harmony, such as shown in the color illustrations on page 20 where *variation* of color rather than contrast of color value is used to express the exhibitor's intent would make a poor black and white print. Many a tricolor winner has learned this to her dismay. The newspaper photographer passed up her arrangement for one more "photogenic." However, the tricolor arrangement must be superior in every respect—the chromatic design as well as the structural design!

The structural design is the most important one, for it determines the extent of the chromatic design which can be superimposed upon it; but it is only a part—not the whole design.

Any structural design may have more than one color design, as shown in the illustrations on pages 18 and 19. In fact, the number of color designs that can have the same structural design is without limit. This is not only true of all design in art, but is true in other subjects, where its dual character is more readily recognized. A piece of furniture, a room, or an automobile, when it is repainted retains its original structural design but receives its second color design.

In floral design we are concerned with two designs—structural and chromatic—and with the separate visual impact of each.

Open Forms — Enclosed Space. The tulip has an open form, consisting of petals which together enclose space.

Line and Form

LINE

Pure line is an extension of a point. It has only one dimension, length.

A line forces the eye to move or travel along its entire length in order to encompass all of it, thereby creating a visual path. The arranger deals with pure line only as *outline*. Pure line is present in the outline of a petal, flower, leaf, stem, container, or background.

Outline delineates form. It marks the limit of an object. This may be the outline of a linear form, shape, open or closed form, or the flat surface on a three-dimensional form.

FORM

Form is the outward contour of three-dimensional material. It is the outward contour of all individual components, as well as of the whole design. In other visual arts, those that depend on *form-less* mediums, such as painting and sculpture, the term "form" is used only to designate the ultimate design. In floral design, however, we are working with a medium in which form is inherent. If the term "form" referred only to the whole design, but not to its components, it would be an objective, not an element. At this point we are interested in the form of the components, rather than that of the whole design.

All forms have three dimensions, but dimensions and relative dimensions vary. All may be grouped under two broad classifications:

1. Linear form—one dimension is much greater than the other two.

2. Contained form—two or all three dimensions are significant.

The force and function of form varies with dimension and with relative dimension.

LINEAR FORM

A form in which one dimension predominates is a linear form. It is much longer than wide or thick. Examples are cattails, yucca leaves, and wisteria vines. The outline of a linear form includes two lines moving in the same general direction.

This type of material is sometimes referred to as spike or steeple material—words which imply stiffness and vertical straightness; however, a linear form may be straight or curved, short or long, thick or thin, and its placement need not be vertical.

Material need not have specific length or thinness to have the attributes of line, but its *relative* dimensions are important—one dimension is much greater than the other two.

A long branch is linear material, but when cut into several short pieces, even though width and thickness remain the same, it ceases to be linear material. A bushy branch can be changed to linear material, without changing its length, by removing side branches.

LINEAR FORM CREATES VISUAL PATH

A linear form forces the eye to move or travel along its entire length in order to encompass all of it, thereby creating a visual path. Observe the lines on pages 111 and 142. Thus **the function of pure line or linear forms in design are the same,** so the terms "line" and "linear form," when relating to their function in design, may be used interchangeably.

The visual path that is created will, of course, vary with the plant material. Observe the lines on pages 90 and 117. The path may be long or short, narrow or wide, straight, angular or curved. If curved, it may curve gently or swiftly. It may close back on itself, either partially or completely, or it may reverse itself. It may be smooth or unbroken, or it may be interrupted by many other lines—visual paths leading off from it—so that its course is poorly defined, and the eye will jump from one path to another in a confused manner. The path may be so bold and well defined that its momentum takes the eye on beyond it leaping across a gap to pick up the course of another line. Visual paths, just as foot paths, can be traveled in opposite directions.

Since lines create visual paths, they are useful where we want the eye to move about in an arrangement.

LINEAR FORMS ESTABLISH STRUCTURAL FRAMEWORK

Linear forms serve to create the skeleton or structural framework of an arrangement.

In a bridge or house, beams are used to form the structural framework. Just as they remain exposed in a bridge, so in an arrangement lines may be emphasized; or as in a house, they may serve as support for an area to be embellished with other material.

Nature often serves as a guide to selection of linear material. Stems from the upper part of a plant or shrub are often suitable for vertical placement. Side branches may be useful for diagonal placement. The lowest branches—since they have grown horizontally before growing upward or downward—are often useful for low placement, or to achieve a horizontal effect.

Flowers that have linear form are limited in number. The following almost complete the list: baptisia, plumed celosia, delphinium, foxglove, gladiolus, larkspur, loose-strife, physostegia, red and blue salvia, snapdragon, stock, thermopsis, tritoma, and veronica. The usefulness of many of them is further limited by the shortness of their blooming season, and by their other inherent elements, particularly color.

We then turn to other plant material. Almost anything having length can be used where a linear form is needed: vines, long stems, leaves, grasses, green or dormant branches, etc.

Plant material should be studied while still in the garden, and before it is cut, as to what kind of path or structural framework it will establish—whether it can be used with little or no alteration or whether much extraneous material must or may be removed so that the visual path will be well defined, and the structural framework otherwise suitable.

Since linear forms establish the structural framework, they are basic to good design.

CONTAINED FORMS

All forms other than linear forms are contained forms. They do not force the eye to move about. There are several variations of contained forms.

SHAPE

Shape is a form that is predominantly two-dimensional. Length and width are significant. Shape is an area, rather than a pathway, enclosed by an outline that contains the eye within specific limits. Since the eye does not need to move about to encompass all of it, a shape allows the eye to rest.

Most leaves are two-dimensional shapes. The silhouette of a three-dimensional form is also a two-dimensional shape. Shapes, including silhouettes, vary in outline from that of a simple rounded leaf to that of an intricate outline, such as a maple leaf, or a cut-leaf philodendron.

Simple shapes allow a passive state of rest. These do not pull the eye in a singular direction, nor do they attract and hold it in one spot. The eye is allowed to wander through the arrangement from one plane to another thereby *allowing* movement from foreground to intermediate or background areas, thus creating visual depth.

Nature combines most flower forms with an abundance of foliage shapes. These allow the eye to rest or move about freely.

SUBSTANCE

When the third dimension or thickness is still somewhat subordinate, it is known as substance. The horticulturist is fully aware of the importance of substance in his specimens. Substance is equally important in floral design.

Examples of plant material in which substance is greater than the average are callas, lilies, foliage of magnolia, begonias, sansevieria and other succulents.

A glass brick has more substance than most glass vases. Ceramic containers appear to have more substance than glass, even when they are actually thinner.

CLOSED FORMS

Closed forms may be solid or hollow, but since we are concerned only with the visual aspect, their third dimension is the significant factor. Examples are: snowballs, hydrangea, marigolds, rosebuds, physalis, peppers, mushrooms, apples, etc.

OPEN FORMS

Open or volumetric forms have depth. Here the third dimension relates not only to the outside dimension but to the space enclosed by the petal or leaf shapes.

A single petal, leaf, or other shape, when curved becomes an open form. Each curved petal of a dahlia results in a small open form; while the curled aspidistra or cecropia leaf is a large open form. Two or more petals or leaves together may surround a single large space, thus creating a large open form. The form of the oriental poppy, and that of the tulip, as shown in the illustration on page 22, results from a number of petals enclosing space together.

Such forms as the iris, agapanthus, Queen Anne's lace, and some lilies, as shown on page 26, and others that *allow the eye to penetrate* combine the qualities of the closed and open forms.

Closed forms have more visual weight than open forms or forms of thick substance; these, in turn, have more visual weight than simple shapes.

Three-dimensional open or closed forms, attract and hold the eye, so are useful where you want the eye drawn to or held.

REGULAR AND IRREGULAR FORMS

Shapes, closed and open forms may be regular or irregular.

Flowers such as snowballs or agapanthus and most fruits are regular in form. Flowers of regular structure may appear regular or irregular depending on the angle from which they are viewed. Trumpet narcissus, lilies, hemerocallis and other similar flowers are regular when placed to be seen "full face," and become irregular when presenting a side view. On the otherhand, there are some regular forms, such as the iris, that always give us a side view, so that for the arranger's purpose they are always irregular. Flowers of irregular structure, such as the orchid or anthurium are always irregular in form.

Regular forms attract the eye for symmetry is perceived quickly but may not hold interest; irregular forms induce a slower response, but may hold interest longer.

INTERMEDIATE AND VARIABLE FORM

Obviously much plant material lies somewhere between any two variations of form set out above. These intermediate forms may take on the function of either. The thick stalk of the snapdragons or stock may be a linear form or a closed form. The sedum rosette combines the flat shape of leaves with thick substance and is half-way between the open and closed form.

Some plant material may assume all variations, depending on the viewing angle. The simple hosta leaf when seen edgewise is a line; when flat, it is a shape. When bent or curved it may be an open form or even a closed form.

The function of these intermediate forms depends on the other forms to which they are related in design.

Space Inherent in Plant Material. The reflexed petals of the lily enclose space completely. Although the lily has some characteristics of the closed form, the effect of the enclosed space is more pronounced.

Space

Floral design is three-dimensional visual art within three-dimensional space.

In design we are not dealing with outer space, or with endless, undefined, intangible space, but with defined space with real, suggested, or visual limits or boundaries.

Space is a structural element and possesses all the attributes of the other structural elements.

THREE KINDS OF SPACE

Although space is a single element, we must consider space as of three kinds:

1. Total space.

2. Space inherent in plant material and other components.

3. Space created within the design.

THE TOTAL SPACE

The total space is defined by the background and its frame. When the background is near and its frame is a physical frame, or a frame of reference, we start with the specific size limitations, i.e., a space that is fixed and predetermined, and we arrange the other elements within this space.

When the background is distant or changeable, and the frame is a visual frame, the space within which we arrange is more flexible, but is still subject to certain limitations. These limitations relate to the perspective of the viewer, and include the size and shape of the surface beneath, the height from the floor, the viewing angle, and the distance from which the design is viewed.

SPACE INHERENT IN PLANT MATERIAL

We have already learned in our study of form that open forms enclose space, such as the petals of the tulip in the illustration on page 22.

Callas and gladiolus enclose space partially; the tulip and oriental poppy enclose space to a greater degree; the standards of the iris are closed almost completely, yet there is sufficient opening so the feeling is always one of enclosed space rather than of a solid. The falls of the iris and the reflexed petals of some lilies and hemerocallis enclose additional areas, in the opposite direction, as may be seen on pages 26 and 31.

Just as with form, all space is three-dimensional, but in design we are concerned with the predominant dimension. Space may be linear; it may be a flat area, or it may have depth.

A palm leaf is composed of many linear forms and *linear spaces* between the linear forms. The wisteria or bittersweet vines may enclose two-dimensional planes, but when spiraling they enclose three-dimensional space. The tulip and oriental poppy, and the curled hosta or canna leaf all enclose three-dimensional or volumetric space. The space between two parallel leaves on the same stem, such as two rose leaves, one above the other, do likewise.

In the container we may find space in the handles of an urn or pitcher, as well as in the opening of the container. Accessories can supply similar examples of enclosed space.

Thus we start with and have but limited control over the total space, and the space inherent in components. However, the space created within the design is entirely within our discretion.

Lines and Outlines of Foreground Components Establish Two-dimensional Space. Exactly the same components are used in each design, and all design elements are organized

in the same manner, except that the direction of one line is changed from the point of support. Spaces of different size and form have thus been established.

FORM VS. SPACE

While dealing with form we start with the individual forms and create the ultimate form of the design. While dealing with space we start with the total space and create the individual spaces within it. Thus, **with form we start with the parts and create the whole; with space we start with the whole and create the parts.**

The ultimate form is created simultaneously as the individual spaces are created. They are not successive steps, with one procedure preceding or following the other.

PLACEMENT OF LINE AND FORM DETERMINES SPACE

Just as the position of the frame determines the size and outline of the total space, so the placement of foreground lines and forms determines the size and limits of spaces.

Lines and outlines determine linear and two dimensional spaces. In the four designs on pages 28 and 29 we have the same background, the same container, and the same plant material. They are exactly alike except that one line leaves the holder in a different direction in each design—yet there is a distinct difference among the four designs. The difference is in the *spaces between* the lines. Thus space is more flexible than line or form, so can be molded or changed more readily.

Straight lines create spaces having straight sides; curved lines establish curved areas; zigzag lines impart their characteristics to the spaces they help to outline.

Two-dimensional shapes can establish three-dimensional spaces. On pages 32 and 33 the character and structure of the partially or completely enclosed spaces are determined by the contour of the leaf shapes that enclose them. The depth or third dimension of any space, depends on the nearness of background areas—whether these be other parts of the arrangement, a predetermined background, or an indefinite area beyond.

The arrangement that has depth of form will also have spaces that have depth. These volumetric spaces are stronger than the flat two-dimensional areas created by line only. Spaces having large areas and distinct outlines are stronger than those of smaller areas or poorly defined outlines. The aspidistra on page 33 creates stronger spaces than the apple blossom branches on page 28. The contained or fully enclosed spaces are stronger than the fluid or partially enclosed spaces.

While placing the foreground elements, within the overall space limitation, we create the space that becomes a part of the design. We organize lines and outlines to create linear, two-or three-dimensional space; we organize form to create volumetric space.

Strong spaces or weak spaces are neither good nor poor in themselves, but we must recognize their force and the function they perform in the design in order to utilize these forces to our purpose. Usually spaces and background areas play a supporting role to plant material and container, which star in the show. The background is the stage, the flower, the actors.

FUNCTION OF SPACE

The function of space parallels that of form. Linear space, since it is outlined by two outlines extending in the same general direction creates a path for the eye to follow; two- and three-dimensional space allows the eye to rest.

COLOR AND TEXTURE OF SPACE

Does space have color and texture?

The color and texture of space is supplied by the background, and other components immediately beyond it. The colors and textures of the background material—whether fabric, wall paper, wood, or other plant material—are now the colors and textures of the spaces between the lines and outlines of the foreground material. In the illustration on page 10 the colors and texture of the background drapery have become the colors and texture of the spaces within the design.

The background color and texture is the visual part of space and as such is an integral part of the ultimate design.

SPACE AS NEGATIVE FORM

Another manner in which space may be considered, is to consider it as negative form. Space is one of the structural elements. Just as the other structural elements—line, shape, and closed forms—are variations of form, so space is a variation thereof. It is negative form.

The petals of the hemerocallis, above, enclose space partially; the reflexed petals, unlike those of the lily on page 26, enclose spaces of varying dimensions. Note that in each case, the bud placement outlines additional spaces.

Space is a "form" since it possesses all the characteristics of form:

1. It has size, which may vary from small to large.

2. It is always three-dimensional and may be predominantly linear, areal, or volumetric; it may be vertical, horizontal, diagonal, etc.

3. It may be geometric or free form; contained or fluid.

4. It has color and texture.

5. It is present in plant material and other components. In fact, a container or a flower such as a tulip, may be either an open or volumetric form or a fluid or partially enclosed space.

Space is "negative" as distinguished from "positive", since:

1. Positive forms come forward; negative forms recedes.

2. Positive forms are tangible; negative forms are intangible.

3. Two positive forms cannot occupy the same space; a positive and a negative form can occupy the same space. In fact, all positive forms are within a larger space.

Having established that space is not a void but an element in design, it follows that space relationships are subject to the same design principles as those of the other structural elements.

32

Two-dimensional Shapes Determine Three-dimensional Spaces. The placement of the aspidistra leaves establishes the form of the spaces between the leaves. The structure of each space varies with the slightly curving contour of the leaves on the left, or the abruptly curving leaves above.

Size

Size is dimension. Every component has three dimensions. Every component possesses the element of size.

Plant material, in relation to flower arranging, can be classified roughly into large, medium, and small. Dahlias and ball chrysanthemums when seven or eight inches across, hybrid hibiscus and summer hydrangea that may be more than a foot or more in diameter, foliage of the castor bean or diffenbachia, are all examples of large material. Feverfew, coral bells, violets, the foliage of spirea thunbergia and Japanese holly are examples of small material. The great mass of garden material is medium in size.

A pure point has no size, no dimension—length, width, or thickness—so it is not an element in design. When a point has dimension, it is a small form and has the same function in design as other small forms. As such it may be experienced individually, as form, or collectively as texture.

Size may be expressed by a number of different terms: strong line, short line, bold form, small form, subordinate form, dominant form, heavy substance. The term "bold' denotes large size in at least two dimensions and well-defined outline or pattern. The arranger and the judge should recognize all these terms as expressing size.

FORCE IN DIRECT RELATION TO SIZE

The force of a form is in direct relation to size. The larger the size, the more impressive the form; the smaller the size, the less impressive.

The forces exerted by line, form, and space, as set out in the foregoing chapters are those of average size garden material. Sizes that are larger than average exert greater forces; smaller sizes exert lesser forces.

Large long lines of flowers and foliage have directional pull of linear forms but in a greater degree. Bold forms not only stop the eye but attract and hold it. As sizes of lines and forms are smaller than average, the opposite holds true. Shorter lines still have directional pull but are weaker, and whereas smaller forms may stop the eye, they do not attract or hold it. In a bold line arrangement the spaces created with these lines are strong spaces. In a mass arrangement silhouetted with leaves such as ferns or huckelberry or flower tips of larkspur, stock, or the like, the resulting spaces will be small and poorly defined, therefore weak.

VISUAL SIZE

We are concerned not only with actual size, but with apparent or visual size. Actual size is modified by:

1. The distance from the viewer;

2. The size of other components;

3. Other elements—color, texture, pattern—inherent in the same component.

It is axiomatic that the farther away from the viewer the smaller the apparent size of a component; the nearer, the larger its apparent size. The large flowers and foliages given as examples above lose their impact of very large size when viewed from a distance. Thus large flowers in large arrangements are suitable for a church or auditorium, while the very small flowers can be used effectively on a bedside tray.

Apparent size is relative. Large hybrid flowers such as iris or delphinium will appear larger when seen along with smaller species, than when seen alone; species, in turn, will seem smaller than when seen alone.

All dimensions of color—hue, value, and chroma—modify apparent size. Red, the advancing hue, and yellow, the highly visible hue, and all colors in which these predominate, will make any hue appear larger than other hues do. White and light values make forms appear larger than other values do. White, because it has the greatest light reflection, appears to spill out over its edge. Intense chromas have the same effect. Very bright colors appear to glow and to cover a greater area than they do in reality.

Medium and coarse textures break up large areas into smaller ones, thus minimizing apparent size. Very smooth or shiny texture increases apparent size. Shiny texture, just as light value, appears larger because it reflects more light.

Bold pattern within a form will increase apparent size. This is as might be expected, for bold pattern is one consisting of colors which increase apparent size, superimposed on large forms.

Since plant material is our medium, the container should usually be smaller than the grouping of plant material. The background, on the other hand, should be larger.

Although line, form, and space exert different forces in design, each becomes stronger, bolder, or more dominant as size in increased, and becomes weaker and subordinate as size is decreased.

Color Factors

An understanding of the nature of color and the factors involved is essential to the analysis of color elements and their function in design.

Color is the visual sensation induced by reflected light rays.

Color as the human eye sees it depends on three factors:

1. Light,

2. A reflecting or a refracting medium,

3. Vision.

Each factor is the basis of a distinct color theory. The study of color can be approached from any one of the color factors.

Light is the source of all color. Light is the basis of the prismatic theory. Both the amount and the kind of light transmitted determine color. This theory is applied in color photography and color lighting.

Pigmentation is the basis of the pigment theory. The chemical composition of the reflecting surface determines color. According to this theory any color can be created by mixing the three pigment primaries. This theory is applied by artists and painters.

Vision is the basis of color psychology. Vision is the interpretation of reflected or refracted light rays through the optics of the eye and through the mind into the sensation of color. Within this theory there are several color systems that are used in industry and in other fields.

The study of any one alone or of all three of the above approaches to color will not give us the complete answer to the use of color in floral design, but a basic understanding of each one is essential before we can analyze color as an element in design.

LIGHT

THE SOLAR SPECTRUM

The light from the sun contains all the visible light rays. Together they produce daylight or white light.

We can determine the light rays and consequently the hues of which white light is composed by separating the rays with the aid of a glass prism.

Light rays are transmitted by means of light waves of different wave lengths. **Each wave length has its own angle of refraction.** All light rays having the same wave length are reflected as the same hue.

Thus a beam of light directed thru a glass prism on to a normally white surface, i.e., one that reflects all hues, is refracted or separated into its component rays with each wave length coming out at a different angle and being reflected as a series of hues. The longest wave lengths are reflected as red hues; the shortest wave lengths as violet. The resulting band of color, starting with red on one end and ending with violet on the other, contains all hues. This is known as the *solar spectrum.*

The bevel edge of a plate glass mirror or the cut of a diamond is also a prism that refracts light into its component rays. The fire in a diamond results from such refraction. Very small particles of water or oil produce the same effect. We see a rainbow after a shower or in the spray of the garden hose when the sun shines on it; or we see the spectrum of colors in a soap bubble or in a thin film of oil on the surface of water. When manifested in other substances it is known as iridescence.

The major colors in the spectrum band are red, orange, yellow, green, blue, and violet. The colors are always in the same order.

In the rainbow, whether in the sky or in the spray of the garden hose, red is always on the outside and violet is always on the inside of the arc.

Sunlight also contains invisible light. These are light rays to which the eye does not respond. These are the longer infrared rays which are refracted on the red end of the spectrum and the shorter ultraviolet rays, on the violet end of the spectrum.

Bending the spectrum and bringing the two ends together produces a color circle. In this circle there are no sharp separations between one color and the next, but rather a gradual change from one to the other. The colors in the spectrum are all pure hues.

REFLECTION OF LIGHT RAYS

Most color, however, is derived from *reflection* of light rays. Air, water, and some solids, such as clear glass, allow light rays to pass through. These have transparency. Gases, liquids, and solids that do not let light rays pass through have opaqueness. These absorb part of the light rays and reflect the rest. The light rays that are *not absorbed,* but reflected are the ones entering the eye where they induce the sensation of color.

Nothing absorbs all the light rays; nothing reflects all. An object that absorbs almost all light and reflects almost none is black. Black is called *saturated* because it has absorbed the greatest possible amount of light. One that absorbs almost none of the light rays and reflects almost all is white. White is called *luminous* because in reflecting all light rays it "lights up" surrounding areas.

A red rose absorbs all the rays from orange through violet, reflecting only the red ones. The blue delphinium absorbs all the rays, except blue, which is reflected.

An object that absorbs *part of all* the light rays and reflects part of all, is gray.

There is no pure black, white, or gray in plant material.

LIGHT INTENSITY

No object can reflect more light than is directed on it, and since color is but reflected light, it follows:

The brighter the light, the stronger the color;

The dimmer the light, the weaker the color;

No light, no color.

We are prone to think of color being present at all time, only that it cannot be seen in the dark. The fact is that in complete darkness, color is absent.

In the theatre all eye focus on the figure in the spotlight on the stage—the area of lightness and brightness—while the bedecked and bejeweled audience is lost in a twilight of shadows. When the auditorium lights go on, however, the attention is immediately drawn to the forms and colors of nearby spectators.

In the theatre lighting has been developed into a science. Not only is intense spot lighting used for optimum effect, but colors and moods can be changed by a change of light.

Lighting is used for effective merchandising in department stores. Most items are lit by diffused lighting of rather high intensity. The jewelry counter, however—whether costume or precious—is always lit with additional lighting, concealed from the spectator, but casting direct light on gems and baubles. This results in a reflected brilliancy, far beyond what would be the result of general store illumination. The result? More women at the costume jewelry department than anywhere else in the store. You can make a "jewel" of your floral design by supplying it with concealed direct lighting. In most art museums each picture is lighted individually. In color photography *intense* lighting is a must.

Bright violet-red phlox that stood out with brilliancy in a late summer garden was chosen for its color strength. When brought indoors, instead of furnishing the anticipated highlight of color in the arrangement, it created a void in the design. In this case a void in its true meaning—a dark hole, a nothingness.

Iris that glisten with touches of gold color on violet in the sunlight become muddy grays under the average light in the showroom and lose all character in a dark nook of the living room. Even the flaunting brilliant orange-red poppies can become a lost cause in the corner of the living room lighted only with one table lamp, or in the poorly lighted church basement.

The exhibitor in a flower show furnishes the pigment, but she is at the mercy of the staging committee who furnishes the amount of color by means of light.

INCOMPLETE LIGHT

Not only the amount of light, but the kind of light, determine color. Daylight and "daylight" lamps have the full spectrum of color, but all other artificial lights do not contain the full spectrum, consequently cannot reflect the full color spectrum. The old saying "Blues fade out at night," is a misstatement. Candlelight, coal oil lamps, gas lights, and incandescent electric lights contain fewer blue rays, so that when objects are lighted with them fewer blue rays are reflected.

Fluorescent lights, which came into being long after the above saying was accepted, are short on red rays, so give off a greenish light, making the average complexion look greenish.

What has all this to do with flower arranging? The amount and the kind of color in flowers depends on the amount and the kind of light. In flower shows this important factor is often neglected.

COLORS CHANGE EACH OTHER

Colors change in the presence of each other. Since the green of a wall or the red of a rose can be seen from any place within a room, we know that light rays that are reflected from them are reflected in *all* directions. These reflected light rays, striking every other object in the room, are again partially absorbed and partially reflected thereby changing the color of every object in the room to some extent.

Although such color changes may seem to be minor, wall colors in a room do change the complexion of the people in it. Flowers, when brought together, as they are in an arrangement, do "give and take" color from each other.

Proof of this is evident when we realize that surfaces in shadows also have color. If we did not receive a color sensation from re-reflected light, all areas which do not receive direct light would be in total darkness. There would be no shadows or indirect light, only direct light areas and totally dark areas.

The above brief analysis is but a small part of the complete story of light as the source of color. It serves however to emphasize the fact that **Light is the source of all color!**

PIGMENT THEORY

Pigment is substance that absorbs a portion of the solar spectrum or of any other light source and reflects the rest. The pigment primary colors are red, yellow, and blue. Theoretically all colors can be created by mixing these three pigment primaries.

The mixing of pigment colors can be accomplished by use of paint, dyes, or printer's ink. In the case of paint or dye, pigment is suspended in a liquid or viscous vehicle which permits actual blending of suspended pigment particles. In the case of printer's ink, mixing is effected by the blending of minute areas of ink.

Pigment color has three qualities or attributes: hue, value, and chroma.

Although the word "color" is used synonymously with the word "hue," color is a general term. It may refer to hue only, but it may also include the attributes of value and chroma. Hue, on the other hand, is a specific term. The colors in the solar spectrum are all pure hues.

Hue is the specific name of a color. It is the first attribute of color.

The three primary hues are red, yellow, and blue. The three secondary hues are produced by the mixing of the three primaries:

Equal parts of red and yellow produce orange.

Equal parts of yellow and blue produce green.

Equal parts of blue and red produce violet.

Thus the three secondary hues are orange, green, and violet. By placing the three primary hues in a triangle, and the secondary hues halfway between the primaries of which they are composed, we have a color circle of the six major hues: red, orange, yellow, green, blue, and violet, as in the color circle illustrated on page 45.

Consider the similarity as well as the difference between this color circle and the color circle made by bending the spectrum.

The number of colors are the same.

The colors are in the same order.

There is a gradual change of colors in the spectrum circle, an abrupt change within the pigment circle.

The terms "purple" and "violet" may be and are often used interchangeably, since both are the result of mixing red and blue pigments. However, if the distinction need be made between the two, violet would be nearer blue on the hue circle than purple, because violet is present in the solar spectrum, while purple represents the area where the red and violet ends of the spectrum meet and overlap.

It is obvious from the spectrum circle that there are hues between the major hues. These intermediate hues can be created by further mixing of adjacent hues.

All hues can be described or designated within the basic color vocabulary of the six major hues. In a 12-hue circle the intermediate hues are designated by the *primary-secondary* connotation. Thus intermediate hues are:

> red-orange,
> yellow-orange,
> yellow-green,
> blue-green,
> blue-violet,
> red-violet.

In an 18-hue or greater hue circle, the first word is the modifying term, the last word is the basic term. These intermediate hues can be expressed thus:
> Yellow-green—some yellow added to green;
> Green-yellow—some green added to yellow;
> Red-violet—some red added to violet; etc.

Black, white and gray are colors that have no hue. They are known as neutral or achromatic colors.

Value is the degree of luminosity. It is the lightness or darkness of a hue. This is the second attribute of color.

A tint is a lighter value. It is the result of adding white to a hue.

A shade is a darker value. It is the result of adding black to a hue.

The attributes of hue and value are shown on pages 46 and 47.

Chroma is the degree of intensity or purity of a hue. This is the third attribute of color.

Tone is reduced or grayed chroma. It results from adding either the complementary hue or neutral gray. The grayed hue resulting from the mixing of two complementaries is in better harmony with plant material than the grayed hue resulting from the addition of neutral gray to a hue.

Intensity and grayness are often confused with lightness and darkness. This is the result of the common practice of using only two words to describe color. We speak of light red or dark green (value and hue) or gaudy red, drab green or muddy blue (chroma and hue) when we should use all three attributes—chroma, value and hue—to describe color. Weak, dark green or light blue of full chroma, express three qualities or attributes of color.

The attributes of hue and chroma are shown on pages 48 and 49.

All variations of a single hue are often referred to as values of that hue. This is not a contradiction of the definition previously given, but recognition of the fact that all variations of a single hue have both value and chroma.

Value may thus be expressed as: hue plus white and/or black. Value as an element is used in this broader sense. It includes lightness, darkness, and grayness.

The pigment theory of mixing pigments to create new colors prescribes how any desired color can be achieved.

It should be pointed out, however, that color reproduction is by no means as constant as the pigment theory might suggest. There are great variations between different mediums, such as oils, water colors, printer's ink, dyes, etc. Even within the same medium, color reproduction is almost never identical. Paint companies, whose "know how" and finances are geared to that purpose alone, recommend that all the paint for a room be bought at the same time (meaning from a single mixing) since different batches cannot be guaranteed to be identical.

The pigment theory approach does not provide the answers to our color problems, simply because we do not create our colors by mixing. We work with colors as nature provides.

If the artist wants to paint a pink rose or carnation, and has only red and white pigment, he can mix the two to get exactly the value of pink that he wants for his rose or carnation. But if we want a pink rose and all we have are white and red roses our knowledge that a mixture of red and white paint, dye, or ink produces pink does not help us in the least. We must go further in our study of color to learn the answer to our color problems.

The pigment theory shows us how all colors are related. This knowledge together with the vocabulary of color as developed within the pigment theory serves as a most useful tool in the further study of color.

COLOR VISION

The last of the three factors involved in the phenomenon of color is vision.

Light rays, pigment color, and reflected light rays can be measured accurately with scientific instruments. Our perception of color, on the other hand, is highly subjective. Since our eyes are the mechanics by which color enters into our consciousness, certain physical conditions enter into our perception of color:

1. Fatigue can dull all senses, including color perception.

2. Color blindness—a condition in which the eye does not translate all light rays into color.

3. Adjustment to light. Since eyes adjust to the amount of light, they automatically adjust to color. If one enters a dark room from a brightly lit one, the room and the colors in it seem dark. The human eye adjusts itself by dilation of the pupils. This admits more of the light that is present and thereby increases the amount of color. The reverse is also true.

4. Adjustment to hue. An intense color will seem less intense after a few minutes of observation. The mind demands the full color spectrum and the eye supplies it where it is lacking. This can be proved by the following simple experiment. Look at the center of a piece of bright red paper for 60 seconds. Then look immediately at a white sheet of paper. You will now see a green image the size of the red one. The eye will have supplied the complementary color, thereby graying the original hue.

5. Adjustment to contrast. Two strong complementary hues present in the same visual field intensify each other, but the colors will gradually appear grayer, and the contrast will be weaker after a few minutes of observation. To prove this lay two oblong strips of paper, one bright red and one bright green, alongside each other in the center of a white sheet of paper under strong light. Fix the eyes on a spot in the center for 60 seconds. Now turn the sheet sideways. You will now see four squares instead of two oblongs. The two areas where the hue remained unchanged, are now considerably grayed. The other two areas where the hue was shifted have now become more intense.

VISUAL COMPLEMENTS

More profound, however, than adjustment to hue and contrast, is the fact that through the above simple experiments we are able to determine true complements, since the mind supplies the complementary hue. From a series of these experiments, using hues from around the circle we can establish a hue circle in which all opposite hues are true visual complements.

In spite of the highly subjective nature of color perception, normal color sensation still offers a sound basis for visual color organization.

VISUAL COLOR SYSTEMS

Although the pigment theory of mixing colors was applied by artists for centuries, it was not they who eventually clarified the *three-dimensional* aspect of color. Based on visual sensation color has been organized into systems having three color dimensions. These systems present an orderly classification of color so that all color can be named, identified and described with precision. The qualities and attributes of color of the artist and painter become the three *dimensions* of color of the color engineer. There are several color systems among them the Birren system and the Munsell system.

In the Birren system[1] the color circle is composed of twelve *standard* hues. The spacing of hues in this system is unlike the equal spacing of yellow, red, and blue, in the 12-hue pigment circle. There are two hues between yellow and red, three between red and blue, and four between blue and yellow. The names applied to the intermediate hues are outside of the basic terminology of the pigment theory. Tints, tones, and shades of each hue are depicted on color triangles, having nine steps each.

Aspects of this system that are of interest to the arranger are the following:

1. Opposite pairs of hues are direct visual complements, since they cancel into neutral gray on a spinning color disc.
2. Color triangles furnish a guide to harmonies of tints, tones, and shades.

The Munsell system[2] is based on a color circle of five *principal* hues and five intermediate hues. The principal hues are red, yellow, green, blue, and purple. Values are represented on a vertical scale on which zero is black, ten is white, with nine degrees of gray in between. Chroma is represented on a horizontal scale with zero as gray and extending to varying degrees of intensity.

Aspects of the system are of interest to the arranger because it takes into consideration the following:

1. Mediums vary in degrees of intensity. The greatest intensity of printer's ink, flowers, or day-glow colors is not the same and the intensity of each varies from hue to hue.

2. The greatest intensity of its ten hues is not always at the middle of the value scale. Yellow reaches its greatest intensity at a higher value or nearer white, and blue-purple at a lower value, or nearer black, than other hues.

These and other color systems are based on different but sound premises. A knowledge of the various systems provides a broad and sound foundation for the arranger's understanding of color.

COLOR INTERVALS

Color intervals are the distances between hues on a color circle and between values and chromas on a color chart. Hue intervals can be technically expressed by degrees of a circle; color value and chroma intervals by numerical steps on a color chart.

However, the arranger is more concerned with the visual difference than with technical degrees or steps, so to the arranger, color intervals are the visual differences between hues on a circle and between values and intensities on a color chart.

Neighboring hues, values, or chromas on a color chart, or those that differ only slightly, have small intervals; those far apart, or contrasting, have great intervals. Examples of small intervals are: yellow-green and green, light blue and very light blue; great intervals are: red and yellow-green, white and dark gray.

Although the pigment theory of three primaries and its resulting hue circle achieved through successive mixing of adjacent hues shows us how colors are related, it can be readily observed that the pigment hue circle does not establish a constant graded series of color steps. The hue intervals from yellow to red are smaller than those from yellow to blue. Those from red to blue are intermediate in size.

No attempt has been made by the author to adhere to any one theory or system. The usefulness of the approach to the flower arranger has been the primary consideration.

The 12-hue circle on the inside back cover will be used in the discussion of hue as a design-element.

EMOTIONAL RESPONSE TO COLOR

The emotional response to color comes as a result of the visual experience. The human race has always associated specific colors with certain situations and is keyed to that response. Thus colors are symbolic. Some of these are:

Blue, associated with the color of clear, still water and of ice, is a cool color.

[1]Faber Birren, *The American Colorist* (1948).

[2]A. H. Munsell, *A Color Notation* pp. 16-20.

Yellow, orange, and red, the colors of sun and fire, are warm colors.

Green, the color of all plant life, is restful.

We have already learned that color perception varies, due to a number of different factors. The emotional response varies even more because it is always modified or determined by the previous experience of the individual.

Red, probably more than any other color, can and does evoke opposite emotions. It is associated with the emotions of hate or anger, or with love; with the warmth of a fireplace or "red flannels," or with danger or communism.

Yellow-green is the color of jaundice or the renewal of hope and life, as exemplified by young growth, in the spring.

Purple may indicate rage, or express royalty.

Magenta is scorned by most horticulturists as the color of "weedy" phlox, but it may inspire a fashion designer when known as "shocking pink."

The scientific color systems have adopted nonemotional names for color to avoid emotional response. The advertising world, on the other hand, has created color names, ad infinitum, such as "gunsmoke," "fudge" or "wild honey," for the sole purpose of creating such response.

Color can be a symbol of a mood, situation, ideology or object. Color *may* be used by the arranger to "speak" to the viewer in the hope that the viewer responds to the language. However, the "message" may not be received by the person for whom the particular color symbol evokes a different response.

In flower shows there are often classes that suggest or demand such symbolic interpretation. The flower show judge should be able to judge such color symbolism and be willing to recognize its merits, whether it evokes her personal response or not.

All of the aforementioned variables to which color vision is subject, as well as the vagaries of emotional response, modify our perception of color. Yet there are certain uniform responses to color which will be analyzed in our study of color as a design element. These constant responses furnish us the necessary guide to the use of color elements.

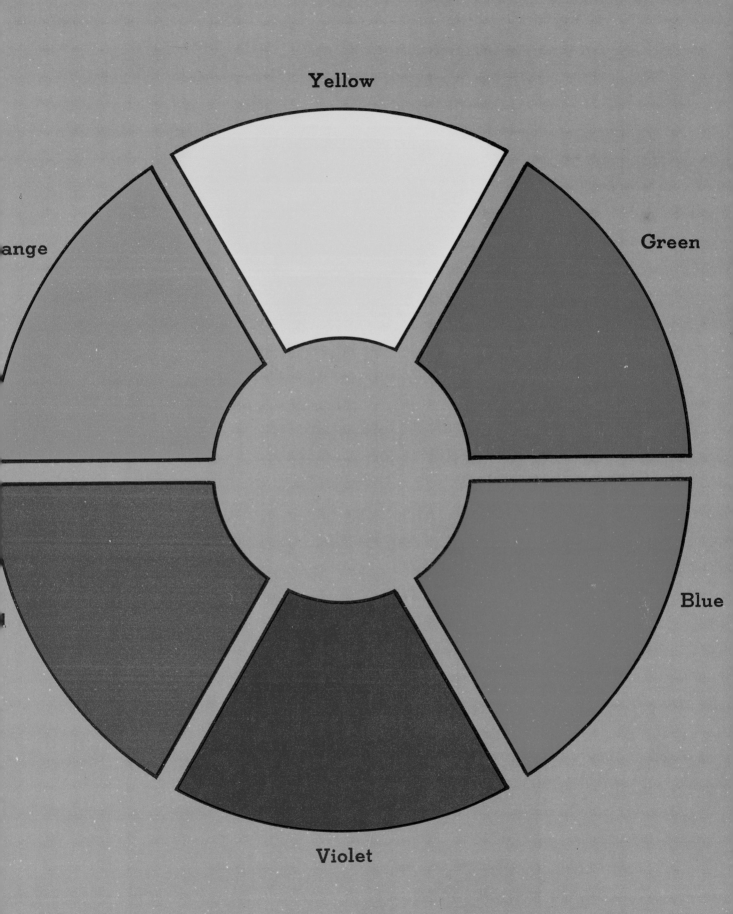

Yellow

Green

Blue

Violet

ange

6-Hue Circle

Hue and

Value Chart

Red	Orange	Yellow

Green Blue Violet Gray

Stimulating
Values

Red	Orange	Yellow

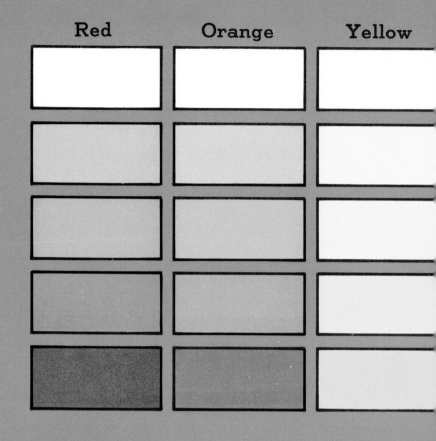

Releasing
Values

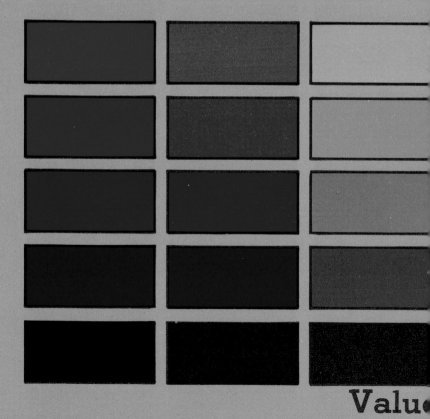

Value

Green   Blue   Violet   Gray

47

Stimulating Chromas

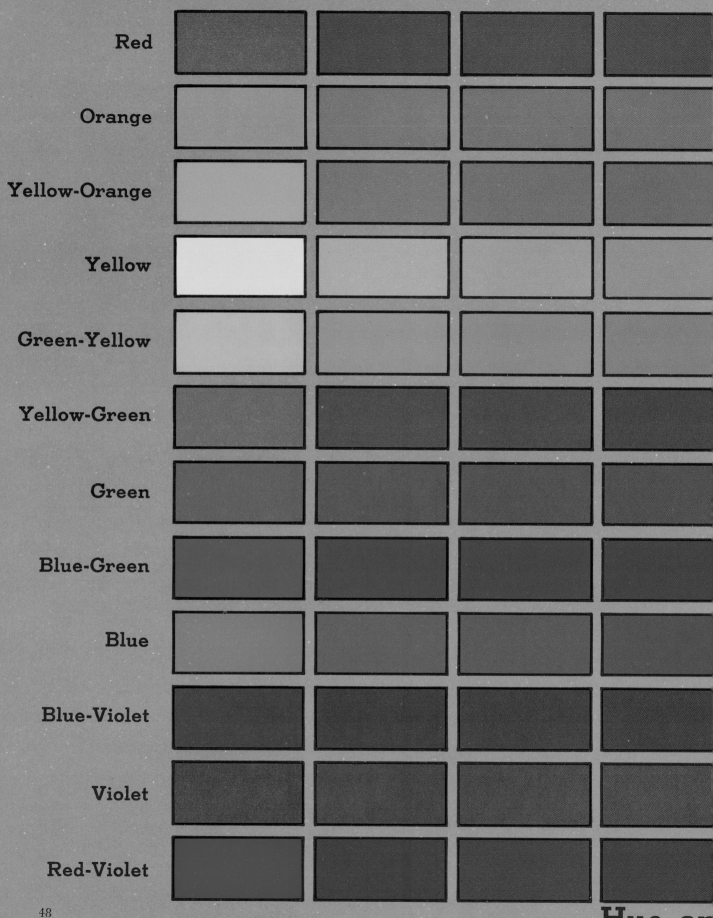

Red

Orange

Yellow-Orange

Yellow

Green-Yellow

Yellow-Green

Green

Blue-Green

Blue

Blue-Violet

Violet

Red-Violet

Hue an

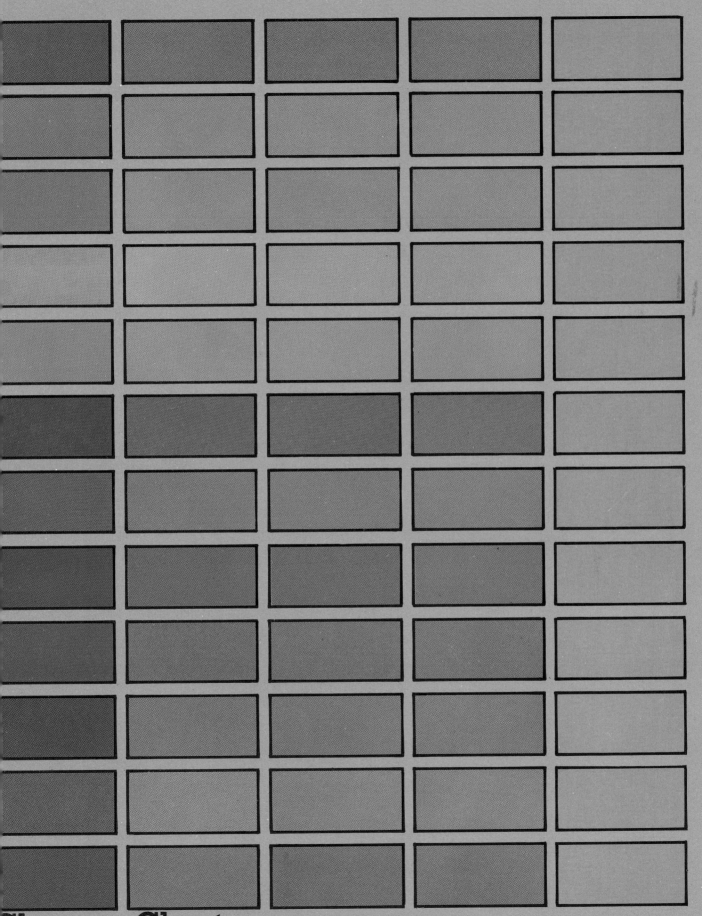

Releasing Chromas

Chroma Chart

Stimulating
Values

Red	Orange	Yellow

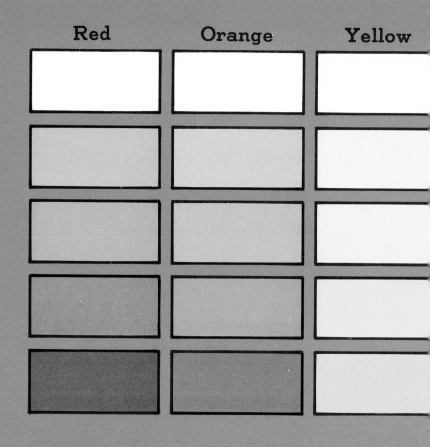

Releasing
Values

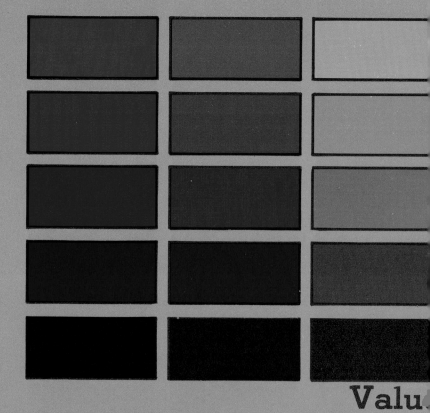

Red	Orange	Valu

Green Blue Violet Gray

Chart

Chromatic Elements

The attributes or dimensions of color—hue, value and chroma—furnish the elements which make up the chromatic design.

In structural design, two-dimensional shapes, open and closed forms are all "forms" because of their similar visual characteristics. They are all "contained."

In a similar manner the attributes of value and chroma are combined in the element of value. All variations of a hue include both value and chroma.

Every color sensation exerts a force upon the mind in some degree. **It is our psychological response to the force of color that determines its function in design.** Our response to color forces guides us in our use of color. These forces vary considerably within each dimension and from one dimension to another. For the purpose of study, however, they may be grouped into two broad categories: stimulating and releasing colors.

STIMULATING COLORS

We have already learned that the amount of light and particularly the amount of reflected light determines how greatly the eye will be stimulated and attracted. The spotlighted stage, the individually lighted painting, the highly illuminated jewelry counter, are examples.

When colors are under the same light, there are some that stimulate more than others. The eye is drawn to these involuntarily. In fact some colors are aggressive. They demand attention and cannot be ignored. This is due to:

1. Inherent chromatic factors in hues.

2. Reflection of most incident light in values and chromas.

ADVANCING AND HIGH VISIBILITY HUES

Let us look again at the three dimensions of color. Within the hue circle on the inside back cover there are advancing hues and receding hues; hues of high visibility and hues of low visibility.

Reds are referred to as *advancing* hues because they appear to be nearer than other hues. Blues are referred to as *receding* hues because they appear to be further away.

Red rays, as they enter the lens of the eye, are only slightly bent; hence they converge or focus at a point behind the retina. To bring red rays into focus, the retina becomes more convex, just as it does to focus on a nearer object. This brings red objects to the same visual distance as nearer objects of static hues. Blue rays, on the other hand, have shorter wave lengths and are bent at a greater angle as they enter the human eye. These rays converge in front of the retina. As the eye compensates by a flattening of the lens, blues appear as far away in the visual field as static hues at a greater distance.

Yellow has the highest visibility; violet, the lowest. These inherent factors enter into and determine what function various hues will serve in your arrangement.

Close your eyes momentarily and then look at the hue circle on the inside back cover again. Which part of the circle attracts your attention first and holds it more? You will note that this portion includes the advancing hues (those in which red predominates) and the highly visible hues (those in which yellow predominates.) The red and yellow hues, as a group, are also known as the warm hues.

Place the chart across the room and repeat the experiment. You will note that the difference is even more pronounced. This experiment can be duplicated with a random spread of color chips or with a random grouping of plant material. A red carnation, an orange poppy, or a yellow daffodil will attract attention and hold it more than a blue cornflower, a purple iris, or a green leaf.

Since the hues from red thru orange, yellow, and green-yellow attract and hold the attention, they are the stimulating hues.

WHITE AND LIGHT VALUES

Note the Value Chart on pages 50 and 51. The middle values have been eliminated to leave only the lighter and darker values. Close your eyes momentarily and then look at the Value Chart. Observe that the upper half that consists of white and light values including light gray will attract and hold your attention more than the lower half. Because white reflects all the rays and light values reflect more light than dark values, this is to be expected. You can enjoy white lilies and moonvine in the garden long after sundown when all hues have become gray.

Since white and light values reflect more light rays, they increase the apparent size of components. A white flower against a black background appears larger than it is and, conversely, a very dark flower against a white background seems smaller than it is.

It is often said that white unites discordant hues. Placing white flowers between two discordant hues does not unite them but makes them less discordant by separating them and drawing attention to itself; however, it often creates a new problem, to unify three discordant colors instead of two. White, therefore, may be a poor choice for a container, because it draws attention to itself—except for use with white or very light-colored flowers.

Since white and light values attract and hold they eye, they are the stimulating values.

STRONG CHROMAS

We return to the chroma chart. On pages 48 and 49 each of the twelve hues is shown with intense chroma on the left and grayed chroma on the right. By repeating our previous experiment, we find that the left portion is stronger than the right. On the left are the strong chromas—each hue at its greatest intensity or brightness.

Since strong chroma means all the rays of a hue reflected, instead of only a part of the rays, the visual experiment proves what might be expected. Intensities vary with the pigment medium—paint, water color, printer's ink, plant material, etc. Pigments developed recently and now used extensively in advertising have a degree of intensity unequaled by any other medium.

Since intensity attracts and holds the eye, intense chromas are stimulating chromas.

Thus we find in each color dimension that there are colors that are more stimulating than other colors in the same dimension. Briefly they can be grouped as: Warm and white, light and bright.

Stimulating color can change negative space into a positive force in design.

Stimulating colors, in each dimension, serve to attract and hold the eye. So place them in your design where you want the eye to be drawn or held.

RELEASING COLORS

Other colors that do not stimulate can be grouped as releasing colors. These colors vary in force from one dimension to another and vary further within each dimension.

RECEDING AND LOW VISIBILITY HUES

Receding hues are those in which blue predominates. The low visibility hues are those in which violet predominates. They are opposite the advancing and highly visible hues. The blues are also the cool hues.

Since blues recede they serve to create a feeling of depth in design. They function to strengthen the three-dimensional effect. Blue larkspur and clematis help to suggest depth in an arrangement.

Violet, because of its low visibility, makes all other hues, by contrast, more visible. Background areas of violet serve to accentuate colors that might be lost against grays or browns. These characteristics of blue and violet are true regardless of the distance at which they are placed.

Due to the atmosphere, green becomes blue-green outdoors, particularly in shadows. All objects or plants are bluish or purplish at a great distance. Thus, both the receding and low visibility hues, not only make the same object appear further away, but enhance the feeling of distance because these colors connote great distance.

STATIC HUES

Green and red-violet are between the advancing and receding portions of the color circle. These are the passive or static hues which neither advance nor recede, are neither warm nor cool, and are of medium visibility. Since green is the color of more plant material than all other hues combined, its design function is of foremost importance.

In our study of the structural elements we recognized that nature combines all flower forms with two-dimensional shapes of foliage. We now observe that nature combines all flower colors with green. Foliage is not only of a static hue, but of middle value and moderate chroma. There is no bright green in nature.

As with two-dimensional shapes, green allows a passive state of rest. The eye is allowed to rest or to wander through the arrangement from one area to another, from one plane to another, and from foreground to background, to allow full impact of depth and space. The eye is neither drawn to nor pulled in a singular direction, but may move freely. Consequently green shapes are useful in successive planes in the body of an arrangement.

DARK VALUES

Dark values are opposite the light values on the value scale. Four characteristics of black and dark values combine to determine their function in design:

1. Have more visual weight.

2. Appear smaller in size.

3. Are unobtrusive.

4. Contain all three primary hues.

Because they appear to have more weight, dark plant material such as coleus, purple leaf plum, dark red croton leaves, or dark red tulips, when used low give stability to an arrangement. When used over the edge of a dark container, they serve to unify plant material and container. Dark areas appear smaller than the same areas of a lighter value. Their apparent smaller size and unobtrusiveness reduces their importance. Dark plant material readily assumes a subordinate role to plant material of stimulating color.

Dark colors are achieved by the addition of black which contains, theoretically, equal amounts of all three pigment primaries. When we add black, we are adding all three primary hues. A dark flower, regardless of its strongest hue, thus contains red, yellow, and blue, and so will be in harmony with a wider range of other plant material than a flower of a lighter value.

THE MULTIPLE ROLE OF YELLOW AND VIOLET

Hues do not all have their greatest intensity at middle value or halfway between light and dark. Yellow, at its greatest intensity, is nearer to white; violet, at its greatest intensity, is nearer black, than other hues. Thus yellow possesses the characteristics of both a highly visible hue and a light value. Like other light values, it appears larger, yet lighter in weight. Violet combines the characteristics of a receding and low visibility hue and a low value. It appears further away, heavier, and smaller.

WEAK COLORS

Between white and black are the middle achromatic grays. Between light values and dark values are the middle values of each hue. Opposite the intense chromas are the grayed chromas.

The middle acromatic grays and the hues of middle value and grayed chroma function equally in design. They are weak and unobtrusive. They do not demand the eye to stop and linger. They allow other elements inherent in the same components to direct the eye. The tips of most flower stalks are grayed, combining green with other hues. These grays still permit the eye to follow the strong linear form. Grays also function well in background areas where you do not want the eye to be held.

The above simple classification might appear to answer all color problems in an arrangement. Two other considerations, however, turn the choice of color into a much more complex problem. These facts are:

1. Each color has all three dimensions.

2. Color is seen only in relation to other colors, never alone.

COLOR MAGNITUDE

Color magnitude is the total force exerted by a color. It is the combined force of hue, value, and chroma, together with texture, multiplied by the area of color.

So in order to determine the magnitude of a color or the total force exerted by it we must take into consideration all three dimensions. Hue, value, and chroma combine forces.

Artemesia, stachys, and mullein are all gray-green, but they are all light in value, so are stronger than many hues, which are darker. We have already observed that blue larkspur and blue clematis serve to suggest depth in an arrangement. But if they are *light* blue, they do not serve the same purpose. Their lightness stimulates. A dark red celosia would be subordinate to a pale lavendar gladiolus or a light yellow-green coleus. A bright green container would overpower an arrangement of dried brown foliage.

COLOR FORCE IS RELATIVE

The strength or weakness of a color is never absolute, as the experiments with stimulating and releasing colors may tend to show, but is always relative.

A color is never seen alone. The eye cannot isolate a color in its visual field but registers all the colors seen at the same time. Any color is seen only in relation to other colors immediately surrounding it or in close proximity. These other colors may be in other flowers, the container, accessories, or in the surrounding space. Flowers in the florist's refrigerator are mostly advancing or highly visible hues, light values, or intense chromas. A red rose, white calla, or a yellow snapdragon will lack force in a sea of others of like hue and value. Take one away from this background of competing color and co-ordinate it with foliage, container, and background of less stimulating color and its color strength is evident.

Flowers in the garden, when seen against their own foliage, which is generally moderate in hue, value, and chroma, may appear strong, but their strength must be reassessed when placed near other flowers in an arrangement. A grayed blue iris that appears weak alongside of a vibrant orange-red poppy can appear stronger when coupled with grayed, blue-green pine. It may even be stronger than red-orange if the red-orange is weak or dark enough. This value could be found in an aged bronze container or in a background of dark brown burlap. Weak material can achieve relative strength by using it with material that is even weaker in color.

In our experiments with the hue, value and chroma charts, we react to color which is shown on a medium gray background. This is equivalent to saying "When other things are equal, or when other colors are middle gray, certain colors will appear strong and others will appear weak." But colors are not always seen in relation to a gray background of middle value.

When the hue and value of the foreground material are nearly the same as the hue and value of the background, the foreground material loses force. Pink is a strong value of a strong hue, but pink flowers in a pink container against pink drapery lose all their strength.

When we are selecting an element, its strength or weakness registers in relation to surrounding colors at the time of selection; however, its final strength or weakness depends on colors with which it is related in design.

FORM PLUS COLOR

The forces of structural elements as set out in previous chapters and chromatic elements may thus be co-ordinated:

1. **Bold forms and stimulating colors attract and hold the eye.**

2. **Linear forms lead the eye; releasing colors allow the eye freedom of movement.**

Form and color, function together to guide the arranger in the placement of material.

FORM vs. COLOR

In some plant material the functions of form and color do not coincide. Examples of such material are: red salvia, with linear form and stimulating color; grayed blue hydrangea or grayed lavender chrysanthemums, with bold form and releasing color.

Of course, this may be exactly what the arranger needs to carry out her contemplated design. Usually, however, material in which the forces of form and color are at odds, presents some problems. We may find it necessary to bring form and color into better relationship.

Form can be changed. Form can be readily changed so that its force is in harmony with its color:

red salvia may be grouped for a change of form and size; blue hydrangea may be separated into smaller clusters; chrysanthemums may be shown with a side view for a change of form.

The color of any one component cannot be changed as readily. Increasing the light will intensify all the colors, not just one. We resort to the fact that color forces are relative, and we combine bold forms of releasing color with other components of weaker color.

CHROMATIC ELEMENTS DEFINE STRUCTURAL ELEMENTS

Although size and form can be determined by the sense of touch, visually they can only be determined by color. All three dimensions of color—hue, value, and chroma—combine to distinguish one form from another. A piece of white paper on another larger piece of white paper cannot be distinguished as a separate object. Its size and form can only be determined if the light is such that the *edge* of the paper reflects more or less light than the surface itself.

In a color print, color transparency, or in a flower show (where we cannot touch an arrangement,) we can determine form and size *only* by color. In each case all three dimensions of color come into play. In a so-called "black and white" picture, hue and chroma have been eliminated, only value remains. These various values of gray, still present, distinguish one form or size from another.

Our "Visual Response to Color" gives us a definite guide to the use of color. It is geared not only to the viewer's visual reaction but to our medium of plant material. It gives us a tool with which we can handle color as an element in any type or style of floral design.

Texture

Texture is surface structure.

Texture is related structurally to form and size, visually to color. Recognizing the relationship of texture to form is essential to understanding the function of texture in relation to color.

FORMS BECOME TEXTURE

How is form and texture related?

In the illustration on page 60 note the gradual change in *size* of the individual forms of flowers, and on page 61 that of foliage. As the size of the individual forms becomes smaller, forms become texture. There is no sharp line between form and texture. Much depends on the distance and viewing angle.

Foliage that is recognizable for its form in an arrangement becomes texture in the landscape. The large foliage of Magnolia grandiflora and the very small leaves of the Japanese hollies have similar texture, color and form. Their textures are smooth and shiny; their colors are dark green; their forms are similar; both have thick substance. Their difference is *size*. In the landscape, however, the latter is known as fine-textured material. From an airplane, a September cornfield can look like green and brown tweed.

The same is true in a photograph of an arrangement. Flower forms that are large enough to be enjoyed as such in an arrangement become merely texture when reduced in size in a picture. Interesting textures, in turn, may become completely obliterated.

The same gradual change from form to texture exists in actual surface structure, such as on the bark of a tree. A very rough, ridged bark appears to consist of narrow forms of a lighter value, superimposed on a background of a darker value. Other bark may appear as forms of one value of brown with forms of another value of brown between them. On a shaggy bark most of the forms are actually separated from its supporting surface. Again the distance of the viewer to the surface determines when forms become texture.

The hydrangea is often referred to as a coarse-textured flower. In reality it is made up of many *small* petals that are not rough in texture but spaced at sharp angles to each other and with their edges toward the viewer.

When forms become so small that we do not experience them individually they become texture.

EMOTIONAL REACTION TO TEXTURE

Our reaction to texture is both emotional and visual. Texture, like the structural elements, can be experienced by both the sense of touch and sight. In floral design, notably a visual experience, it would seem that the actual sensation of touch should not be too important. But we are so conditioned to the fact that certain textures cause specific physical reactions, that their visual image, even without physical contact, immediately creates an emotional reaction. At times it is difficult for us to separate the physical sensation of touch from its purely visual aspect. This is particularly true while we are in the process of arranging and in physical contact with plant material.

We remove the prickles along the rose stem before handling it; the thistle and teasel must be handled with gloves; the mahonia, though glossy textured, leaves a lasting stinging sensation from contact with its needle-like leaf tips. Even the viewer may be repelled by a spiny surface. On the other hand a satiny texture invites us to experience its surface by reaching out and touching it.

Form to Texture. Starting with large forms of flowers, as above, or foliage as on the right, and proceding clockwise, forms gradually become smaller until they appear to be texture. There is no sharp distinction between form and texture. When forms are so small that we do not experience them individually, they become texture.

Velvet-y, satin-y, down-y, fur-ry, are so named because they conjure up sensations of these substances, together with their past associations: velvet and satin — richness and formality; down and fur — animal warmth and coziness.

Our emotional reaction is the result of previous physical experience.

The important difference between the emotional reaction and the visual impact is that the former *may* influence design, the latter does influence it. The former may be evoked in interpretive or expressive design, the latter is important to all design.

DUAL ROLE OF TEXTURE

As an element texture must be considered in two respects:

    1. As a primary element.

    2. As a modifying element to that of other elements.

TEXTURE AS DESIGN ELEMENT

Very smooth and very rough textures are *both stronger* than in between textures.

The texture of shiny unbroken surfaces is strong because there is greater light reflection from them. Rough textures are strong because the sharp contrast of light and dark areas defines these areas so that many small forms are recognizable. Thus both the very smooth texture of glazed ceramic and the very coarse texture of tree bark are stronger than the in-between textures of most foliage — but for different reasons.

Smooth textures attract attention, but rough textures may hold the attention longer. This is so because in the first case the story is told so quickly; in the second, having crossed the line from texture to recognizable form, the eye must wander over the area to encompass all it has to offer.

But the most important texture of all is the in-between texture of foliage. The inherent elements in foliage are not only intermediate forms and static colors, but the in-between textures, all of which are passive and restful. Indeed, foliage is the great harmonizer in nature—and it serves the same purpose in design.

LIGHT ANGLE CHANGES TEXTURE

Light coming from the same direction as that of the viewer casts its shadows beyond so that the surface will appear to be relatively flat.

Light from the left will cast strong shadows to the right. The same holds true for light coming from above, below or from the other side — each casts shadows to the opposite direction. The surface projections create the shadows, but where these shadows will be and how deep they will be depends on the *angle of light*. We learn from the portrait photographer that light from several directions serves to minimize shadows. The arranger may want to control the light angle to emphasize texture, or to use several light sources to minimize texture.

HIGHLIGHTS

Wherever the viewer and the source of light meet at equal angles on a smooth, glossy or shiny surface, there will be almost a complete reflection of light. This area which appears to be more highly illuminated than surrounding areas is known as being highlighted. These spots, areas, or lines of greater brilliance give life and luster to a surface.

On metal, especially silver, or any other highly polished surface, these highlights may be so strong that they catch the eye and distract it so that all other areas seem dull in comparison.

On the other hand, a dull surface, which does not reflect highlights, may be so lifeless as to be depressing. Many ceramic manufacturers have attempted to make containers with very dull surfaces on the theory that these were most suitable for flowers. Yet these containers seldom enhance an arrangement.

Minor highlights on the surface of a container, together with the variations in color value that these create, give "life" to a container without the container overpowering the arrangement.

A question frequently asked is "Should we never use a silver container?" If you place flowers in a tall silver vase in the living room, chances are that the silver vase has the strongest highlights of any object in the room, and that the container will be more dominant than the flowers. Flowers in a silver container on the dining room table present a different situation. The container is more likely to be a low one, and the light

A Study in Texture. In the assemblage, on the right, the plumed cane, almost silky to the touch, appears to have a rough texture. The surface of the pressed wood, although very smooth, is visually a rough texture. Both are due to the strong variation and contrast of value. Note the highlights on the bottle and jug resulting from the light reflection from their slick surfaces.

source is from an angle that does not reach all of the container directly. The container is only a part of an overall pattern of silver found in the table flatware or other appointments. Consequently a silver container may be a poor choice for one purpose, an excellent choice for another.

Under direct light, such as an overhead chandelier or candles, the stimulating colors — white and light values and/or strong chromas of the red through yellow hues — are usually strong enough for use with silver. The releasing colors — grayed and dark values of blue, purple, green or brown or likely to be subordinate to the highlights of silver.

TEXTURE AS A MODIFIER

As a modifying element, texture does two things:

1. It breaks up large areas into small ones, thereby modifying form and size.

2. It creates many small shaded areas which are grayer, thereby modifying color values.

Texture modifies size. Two areas of exactly the same size but different textures will appear to be of different size. The very smooth unbroken area will appear larger; the textured, coarse area will appear smaller. The crackled ceramic vase will appear smaller than the shiny silver one.

The visual difference in size may seem to be of minor consideration in selection of components, but we learn from other fields of experience of the importance of this visual difference. A woman looking for a dress that will make her look smaller does not select a shiny satin, a light color, or a large-flowered one. Instead she looks for dull textures, dark colors, and small prints.

TEXTURE MODIFIES COLOR VALUE

Since color is reflected light, the physical structure of the reflecting surface has its impact on color. The smooth, unbroken surface will have direct reflection of hues. This allows hues to be perceived at full intensity. Surface projections stop light rays from striking areas immediately beyond thereby casting many minute shadows. Shadows, which are areas not in direct light, receive only re-reflected light (previously discussed under the light factor of color.) This is always less

than direct light. Shadowy areas are thus grayer and weaker in color. If a piece of wool and satin are dyed in the same dye bath, the textured wool will appear to be gray alongside of the shiny satin. A coarse texture, by creating dark shadows, is equivalent to adding gray to the hue.

TEXTURE MAY INTENSIFY CHROMA

Very rough textures, those that create deep shadows which are nearly black, will serve to give a contrast of chroma, and make hues more intense.

This seeming contradiction is understood when we remember that we have crossed the line from texture to form. When surface projections are minute there is a merging of hue and grayed hue so that the entire area will appear grayed. When the projections are large enough to be recognized as individual forms, the hues or values of each stand out separately and these are then intensified by contrast.

The impact of texture on color is as important as its primary consideration of surface structure.

COLOR AS VISUAL TEXTURE

When color areas are too small to be discerned as areas of color, we respond to them just as we do to small forms. A smooth surface that is stippled, mottled, or marbled will evoke the visual response of a textured surface.

Where the variation is one of value only, within the same hue, the effect is even more pronounced. Variations of value in minute areas is similar visually to variations created by texture. This is to be expected, since texture modifies value but does not change hues. The variations of green on the sansevieria leaves on page 101, as well as the variations of gray on the container give a heavily textured effect even though both are actually shiny. In the design on page 63 the variations in value in the pressed wood create a coarse visual texture, even though the surface is quite smooth.

Rough texture or smooth texture, or any other texture, is never good or poor per se. Instead we are concerned with the force any given texture exerts in relation to other textures in the design.

TEXTURE vs. OTHER FACTORS

Texture is often confused with other factors. It is not substance, nor quality, nor price, and it bears no relation to the previous company it has been keeping.

Substance is thickness and third dimension. The greatest impact of texture is on color value; that of substance is on visual weight.

Glass can have the same texture whether it is thick or thin; the difference is substance. Smooth, shiny, glossy, sandy, rough, coarse, bristly, or dull, all describe texture. Thick, thin, solid, transparent, succulent and heavy, all describe substance.

The word "fine" is often used to express good quality, or high cost. It does not necessarily follow that the same article has fine texture.

Traditionally, a lace or embroidered cloth, "fine" china, greenhouse roses in a silver bowl represented the costliest items that money could buy. They "kept company" for so many years that they seemed to belong together.

The lace cloth, however, may be coarse. "Fine" china does have a very smooth texture, but fine textures are often also found in inexpensive items. A plastic dish, in substance as thin and translucent as "fine" china, may have an even smoother texture. A polished aluminum container and a silver one may have exactly the same texture, and even the same color.

The petals of a rose are no finer textured than the petals of a sunflower; and the thorns on a rose are hardly fine-textured. Greenhouse flowers are often re-ferred to as finer, more delicate and fragile than garden flowers. The opposite is more nearly the truth. Only "toughies" live long enough and can survive the wholesale harvesting, long distance shipping, numerous handlings, and changes of temperature that commercial flowers receive, and still came up looking fresh and turgid. The toughest flowers are indeed the orchids and exotics. As a class the woodland wildflowers are probably the most fragile of all.

The above table appointments constitute a "traditional relationship" brought about originally by cost and not by similar textures.

The dictionary defines formal as "in accordance with scrupulous observance of social forms, customs, and etiquette." For formal or semi-formal dining tables we may adhere to these traditional relationships. For informal tables the continual trend has been away from the traditional toward harmony of table appointments based on their form, color and texture.

As floral design has evolved we have broken away from formerly accepted prejudices. There was a time when flowers were put only in "vases." Our forebears would have been puzzled to see flowers in driftwood (a piece of old wood to them,) in the lampbase, the beanpot, the sugar bowl, the coffee grinder, or in the dustpan. The contemporary arranger considers these "containers" only in terms of form, color, and texture, and not in terms of previous function or original cost.

Since texture modifies color value more than it does any other element, it may be considered as part of the Chromatic Design.

Pattern

Pattern is the silhouette created by a combination of lines, forms, and/or colors, and the spaces between them. It is present in plant material as well as in the ultimate design.

Pattern is not a *single* element. It is the result of a combination or grouping of elements, such as a combination of lines, shapes, open and closed forms, and the resulting spaces between and around them. Or it may be a combination of colors. These may be of the container, background, but particularly of plant material.

The arrangement of leaves on the stem, the order of petals on a blossom, the branching of smaller stems from a larger one, the gradation from bud to open flower on a spike, are all patterns of plant material.

A session on judging horticulture will verify the fact that the horticulture judge expects to find well organized patterns in plant material. The following are random notes from various horticulture scale of points: branching habit, character of spray, style and grace, beauty of plant form, branch and bud placement, and habit of inflorescence.

Pattern may be a design within a design, a portion of a larger design, or a partial design not complete in itself. **But since these combinations are inherent in plant material and cannot be resolved into their respective elements, the combinations or patterns must be considered as units, for design purposes.**

We have already observed that line, shape, form, space, size, hue, value and texture serve to attract, stop, hold, move, or rest the eye in varying degrees. Patterns within a form, space, or color create additional variations of this function. Patterns within a shape, form or space may be color patterns or they may be structural. The variegated hosta is a color pattern on the leaf form. The pattern within a bunch of grapes is due to structure. The pattern on a caladium leaf is a color pattern that follows the structural pattern, as evident in the illustration on page 68.

MASSED PATTERNS

Massed patterns are those in which the pattern in any area, whether in the center or on the outside, is similar to any other area. Examples of massed patterns are geraniums, hydrangeas, snowballs, carnations, etc. Since many of the massed forms are really an inflorescence of many small flowers, two or more can be grouped to create larger forms, portions removed to make smaller forms, or small individual flowers bunched to make a large form, all without changing the inherent elements, except size.

REGULAR PATTERNS

Regular patterns may be concentric, converging or a combination of both.

Concentric patterns are made up of progressively larger circles, such as in a full blown rose.

Converging patterns are made up of lines converging to a central point, such as that of a clematis or daisy.

Concentric patterns increase the stopping power of simple circular shapes and forms. Converging patterns add the force of converging lines. Dahlias and large flowered zinnias combine these patterns to be effective "eye stoppers."

Just as the viewing angles can change a regular form into an irregular form so the pattern within a form may change from a regular to an irregular pattern as the viewing angle is changed.

Color Pattern Follows Structural Pattern. In the caladium leaf the white and green color pattern follows the structural pattern created by the framework that gives physical support to the leaf.

IRREGULAR PATTERNS

Most irregular forms have irregular patterns within the form. The irregular structure as seen in the side view of the iris has an irregular pattern. The asymmetrical begonia leaf has an asymmetrical pattern.

The placement of petals within a flower, i.e., the pattern within a form determines the design function of the flower. A regular flower such as the dahlia, having both a concentric and converging pattern with petals converging at the center, attracts and draws the eye irresistably to the point of convergence, but interest may not be sustained. On the other hand, an irregular pattern within an irregular form, such as the iris or orchid, may not attract the eye quickly but will hold it longer.

As might be expected, there is similarity in our reaction to form, texture, and pattern. Regular forms and patterns and smooth textures attract, but interest may not be sustained. Irregular forms and patterns and rough textures may not attract the eye as quickly, but will hold it longer.

PATTERN AND FORM

Because of pattern, linear forms, shapes, open and closed forms are not as clearly defined as a first analysis may indicate. A single piece of plant material can have all variations of form or may be intermediate between any of them.

The elongated buds at the tip of a gladiolus are linear in form; the open florets at the bottom are open forms; those between are intermediate. All florets are arranged in a pattern along the stem so that the form of the entire stem is linear.

Individual pine needles are linear in form; as shown in the illustration on the right they are grouped in a pattern that creates a cluster that is intermediate between an open and closed form; but the pattern of the intermediate forms on the branch brings the entire branch back to a linear form.

A branch of weigela poses the following: the individual florets are open forms, and though regular, usually present an irregular form; they are grouped in a pattern that is intermediate between an open and closed form; the foliage up and down the stem has simple shape. Both the intermediate flower forms and the foliage shapes are arranged in a pattern on the stem which makes the branch taken as a whole linear in form.

Pattern of Lines. The lines of the pine needles establish a pattern in each cluster. The clusters establish a pattern along the linear branch.

Pattern of Form and Space Inherent in Plant Material, above, Becomes Part of the Pattern of Form and Space in the Ultimate Design, on the right.

Inherent Relationships. Note repetition with variation in both flowers and foliage, and the contrast between them.

Patterns Within a Form and Forms Within a Pattern. Here are patterns in each
leaf form; and patterns of forms and intervening spaces, both in the sprays of
berries, and in the entire branch.

Although much plant material has a simple form this same relationship of form and pattern is evident to some extent in all plant material.

PATTERNS OF FORM AND SPACE

Pattern complicates the relationship of form and space. There may be forms and spaces in a pattern, spaces and patterns within a form, or forms and patterns within a space.

Consider, for example, a hollyhock stalk. The petal of each flower has shape. The shapes of the petals and the spaces between them establish a pattern within the flower. Each flower has form and the flowers are "spaced" (have spaces between them) in a pattern on each stalk. Each stalk has form and these are grouped with spaces between them in a pattern on a plant. Or they may be organized into a pattern to create spaces between the stalks and other material in the arrangement. The resulting arrangement has form.

The same holds true for foliage. The leaflets of the mahonia leaf, as shown on page 70 have form. The leaflets are arranged with spaces between them in a pattern within the leaf. The spaces between the edges of the leaflets are as much a part of the pattern as the leaflets themselves. Again the mahonia leaf has form and the leaves are "spaced" in a pattern along the stem. The entire branch has form and this is combined with other material as shown on page 71, creating spaces between them, in a pattern in the ultimate design. The ultimate design has form.

The pokeberry illustrated on the left shows the pattern of ribs within the leaf; the pattern of berries on the stem; and the pattern of the leaves, berries, stems, and the spaces between them.

PATTERNS OF COLOR

Color patterns may be within a form, such as the pattern on the pink and white camelia, or the multicolored coleus leaf. Or the color pattern may be superimposed on the structural pattern, as on the single caladium leaf shown on page 68, or as the vibrant hues and subdued greens on a branch of azalea.

CONTAINER PATTERNS

Although many containers are simple in form, the same compounding of form and space into pattern holds true as in plant material. An urn, when viewed from the side, is a pattern composed of the closed form of the bowl, which together with the two linear forms of the handles encloses space. The stem and base are intermediate forms and together with the bowl create a pattern which includes additional space.

In the container on page 74 is a pattern consisting of the linear form of the handle, the open forms of the lid, bowl, and base, combined with one large and many small spaces enclosed therein.

The interesting form of many abstract containers comes from the pattern of form and space within the container.

At the time we are selecting the design elements we are concerned with the pattern inherent in the individual components. At the time we are organizing the elements, we are concerned with the pattern of the whole design.

INTERDEPENDENCE OF ELEMENTS

Even though design elements can be and are treated as separate and individual factors in a design, they are closely related and interdependent, each being acted upon and, in turn, acting upon the others.

Color, its hues and values, define line, form, and size.

Line and form define space.

Size distinguishes form from texture.

Size changes color areas to texture.

Texture modifies color values.

Pattern may be within form, space, or color.

Pattern may be of form, space or color.

The interdependence of one element upon another and their basic relationship is established. Although we continue to consider the elements as individual entities, an understanding of this basic relationship is helpful to effective observation.

Patterns of Lines, Forms, and Spaces in a Container. The open form of the bowl and lid enclose one large space. The pattern of the lines and spaces of the handle, and the open form of the base which outlines smaller areas add interest to the design.

Harmony. Note that the pattern of the container suggests the placement of the plant material in it. The plant material serves to enhance, not obscure, its basic design.

Evaluating The
Container and Background

THE CONTAINER

The container is selected for its structural and chromatic elements.

Since the container acts as a visual base or a supporting component to the plant material, a good container should appear to have structural strength—even greater than the plant material itself—but at the same time be subordinate to it. A dark container of good substance, but small size, can meet these seemingly contradictory requirements. A dark container will support more or taller material than one of light value.

I have two containers that are identical in size, form and texture. One is grayed dark red; the other is bright, light yellow. The grayed dark red container combines equally well with red-violet dahlias, violet-red cockscomb, lavendar chrysanthemums, and purple-leaf plum, as with orange-red dahlias, reddish brown coleus, and brownish-red castor bean foliage and seed pods. It is a "good" container and is used frequently.

Three factors combine against the bright, light yellow container. It appears too light in weight, is strong in hue, value, and chroma, and contains only one hue. The yellow container is never quite right. Its usefulness is limited.

The size and form of the container is usually more rigid and fixed than that of plant material. Its form cannot be altered by snipping a piece here or bending a part there. It is usually used "as is." Its unyielding form may dictate to some extent what may be used in it.

Color and texture can be changed more readily on the container than in plant material. A container that has good form may still be a "poor" container because of surface coloring or texture. Painting it can change both color and texture in one operation.

The antique vase with an elaborate scene painted on it can become a dull neutral surface. The brightly-colored raised design or encrusted flowers on the surface of a vase can be changed from dominant forms to rough texture—merely by painting the whole vase in one color. Eliminate color differences and attached forms become texture. On the other hand, visual texture can be created on an otherwise smooth container by variation of value as in the illustration on page 101, or by variation of hue or value, such as may be obtained by stipling.

The clear glass container presents singular problems all its own. Because of its transparency, it may appear lighter in weight than a ceramic container of the same size and substance. Usually it will support less plant material than a similar opaque container. It may leave mechanics awkwardly exposed.

The visual effect of the glass container varies with the amount of light and its direction. With light from above, a dark table may impart visual weight to a shallow container, or its wood pattern may enrich the design. Colors reflected from other surrounding objects or surfaces may impart color to the glass.

In a tall container everything within it becomes a part of the vertical design. Light on forms or colors beyond it, makes them visible through it. The curved glass surface modifies them by distortion and adds them to the visual pattern.

A globular or cylindrical container, filled with water, will act as a magnifying glass. It will increase the size of the plant material in it and dilute its color. Because of magnified size and diluted color underwater arrangements often appear overstuffed with insipid colored material. Mechanics will also be enlarged.

Space is as important in the container as in that portion of the design created with plant material. In the containers on pages 28, 74, 142, and 162, the space under the container contributes to the design by reducing the apparent weight of the container without reducing its size.

Effect of White Background. Compare the effect of the white background on the left with that of a background of lower value on the right. Note that the white background makes the magnolia branch appear thinner, thereby weakening the entire structural design. Furthermore, although the spaces appear larger, they do not appear stronger.

Transition. The heavy linear form of the tulip leaves give transition from the slender vertical line to the open form of the tulips.

THE BACKGROUND

In selecting the background we need only be concerned with its color and texture and overall size, since the spaces or negative forms are created later while the design is being organized.

When background colors are darker, grayer, or more receding, and textures weaker than foreground components, the eye is not drawn to them. It focuses instead on foreground planes, and the background remains in the background.

When background colors are more stimulating, and textures stronger, than foreground components, the eye will be drawn to them.

Hues containing red or yellow, light values, strong chroma and/or shiny textures are just as stimulating in the background as in plant material and container. A shiny bright red satin background is stronger than any plant material you may place in front of it. Your eye is drawn to it first and will go back to it again and again. Red, being advancing, will appear nearer to the plant material and will decrease the depth of an arrangement.

If the background is highly illuminated it will have the same effect as one of higher value or stronger chroma.

White or light backgrounds will make the spaces created in the design seem larger than they are, the forms seem smaller and the lines therein thinner and weaker. Note on page 76, how the white background has reduced the strength and substance of the structural design.

Since color with its three dimensions defines form, a background of the same hue, value, and chroma as the foreground components would weaken foreground forms by obliterating their outlines, and consequently also weaken background areas. An all medium green foliage arrangement in a green container against a dull green background would result in a weak structural design and uninteresting spaces.

Some contrast in hue, value, chroma, and/or texture is essential so that lines, forms and resulting spaces are defined.

However, just how strong or weak the foreground or background areas should be in relation to each other, will depend entirely on the purpose of the design and the intent of the arranger.

PERCEPTION DEVELOPS

The arranger and the judge both gain perception from the practice of evaluating material wherever found: plant material in the garden, in the field, or at the florist; containers in the shop window, department store, or at the flower show; fabrics, walls, woodwork or paper as backgrounds.

Analyzing arrangements at the flower show and resolving them into their elements is a rewarding endeavor. The finished arrangement should be ignored at this point, only the design elements of each component should be studied. An effective way to do this is to list each piece of plant material, the container, background, and accessory, if any. Follow each with a statement of its size, form (line, shape, substance, open, closed, or intermediate,) color (hue, value, and chroma) and its texture. This training will develop an observing eye.

After the arranger or judge becomes thoroughly familiar with and understands the forces and possibilities of design elements inherent in plant material she will be more perceptive and will "see" much that the untrained eye does not see, and discovery will become an exciting experience.

SELECTION CONTINUES

The process of evaluating does not stop when the material is assembled—it continues throughout construction of the design. We continue to decide how much organized pattern to retain, how much to change, or how much to eliminate.

As we organize material we become more aware that *everything is relative*. The rose that appeared to be just the right size and color in the garden may now be either too large or too small, or too pink or too yellow, in relation to the other elements. The dormant branch that was to furnish the dominant line may now be either too thin or too short in relation to the large leaves and bulky container. The pine branch, with its interesting pattern of needle clusters, may create confusion when added to a grouping of other linear material. The process of selection and evaluation of elements and preorganized pattern thus continues until the last component is in place.

Armed with knowledge of the forces and function of design elements we can now select with a purpose and we are now ready to organize potential design material, in a container, within a given space.

PART THREE

INHERENT RELATIONSHIPS

PRINCIPLES OF DESIGN

REPETITION and VARIATION

CONTRAST

SCALE

PROPORTION

DIRECTION

Principles of Design

Design is the organization of visual elements. Having analyzed the components in terms of design elements, the second important step in creating floral design is organization of these visual elements.

We have already observed that every design element exerts a force that determines its function in design, and guides us in its use. Two or more elements brought together create relationships which exert additional forces. However, not all relationships, existing or created, between elements are good. Not all designs are good. They may be good, poor, or indifferent. Thus an analysis of these additional forces is essential.

DESIGN PRINCIPLES

Principles of design are fundamental precepts based on natural forces.

Flower arranging principles are based on design principles which are true for all visual arts. These, in turn, are based on natural forces which act on us and to which we respond. This holds true whether or not we recognize them or understand them. They have always been, and will always be, with us, so we cannot abolish them or ignore them. Now and then some great scientist or teacher has determined what these forces are and has put them into words.

A design principle, when applied to design elements, induces an aesthetic appeal. Thus, design principles serve as guides to aesthetic design.

We can rely on these natural forces to guide us, whether our design is restrained or luxuriant, conventional or creative. We use them to modify design already present in plant material and thereby enhance it.

There are no rules governing aesthetic design, only principles. The only rules to which a flower arrangement is subject in a flower show are the rules determined by the membership of the sponsoring organization. These include the permanent rules and regulations, and those current rules applying to the immediate show at hand, as set out in the schedule. The exhibitor accepts these when she makes an entry in a show.

APPROACHES TO PRINCIPLES

Relationships in floral design can be and should be approached from several perspectives. From each viewing point we can examine each relationship, and thereby arrive at a broader conception of design principles than a single approach could afford. These perspectives are:

1. Inherent vs applied.

   a. Inherent relationships—those that are always present and consequently must be controlled.

   b. Co-ordinating principles — those that must be applied to co-ordinate the forces of the inherent relationships.

2. One unit vs. two or more.

   a. Design relationships that exist within one unit, or within a grouping of material considered as a unit.

   b. Those that exist between two units.

3. Scope of principles. During the process of organizing elements in floral design, we are always concerned with two distinct problems, which must be resolved, consciously or subconsciously:

   a. Magnitude—how much or how many elements or components? How much of this or of that? How large? How long? etc.

   b. Placement—where to place elements or components? to the left? further to the right? higher? lower? etc. Some principles deal with magnitude, others bear on placement.

INHERENT RELATIONSHIPS

The inherent relationships are: proportion, direction, repetition, variation, and contrast. These are the relationships that are always present in:

The medium of plant material, and in all other components.

Every grouping of plant material.

Every design.

RELATIONSHIPS WITHIN ONE UNIT

The relationships that exist in one unit are proportion and direction.

Proportion is the relative size, dimension, or magnitude of one part to another, or of one part to the whole.

Direction is the relative position in space of one element in regard to:

1. Its starting point.

2. Any other point within a unit.

Proportion and direction exist within every unit, whether the unit is an element, a component, a random grouping of any two or more of them considered as a unit, or an organized design.

We can never eliminate proportion or direction; we can only modify or change them.

We are indebted to Einstein for the theory that all things are relative—nothing is absolute.

RELATIONSHIPS BETWEEN TWO UNITS

There are only three basic ways in which any two elements, or components can be combined: complete repetition, complete diversity, or a combination of repetition and diversity.

Exact and complete repetition of all characteristics of plant material does not exist in nature. There are no two pieces of plant material with perfect likeness. We are concerned here with *essential* likeness of all elements.

Repetition of two components means all elements alike except their position in space.

Diversity is the state of differing essentially. Diversity means essential difference, not only of all visual aspects, but of other aspects of components, such as use, vitality, etc. A glass of water and an elephant would represent complete diversity. Between these two extremes there are infinite possibilities of combinations of likeness and difference. These combinations may be classified into two broad categories; variation and contrast.

Variation is a combination in which there is more likeness than difference.

Contrast is a combination in which there is more difference than likeness. Contrast exists only between elements or factors that have a common denominator. The elements or factors are different attributes of subjects that are in some way related. Examples: hot and cold are both attributes of temperature; long and short, of dimension; light and dark, of value.

Since plant material and container furnish the common denominator in floral design, contrast, rather than diversity, is the relationship with which we are usually concerned. It is possible, however, that an accessory or feature might present diversity rather than contrast.

Repetition or variation or contrast exists between the elements of any two components, and consequently, one or all are inherent in every random grouping of two or more components, or in every organized design.

CONTROL OF INHERENT RELATIONSHIPS

Since proportion, direction, repetition, variation, and contrast are always present, each must be controlled to induce its own aesthetic appeal and to achieve its own contribution to good design.

When thus controlled mere relationships become design principles.

SCOPE OF INHERENT PRINCIPLES

In general, repetition, variation, and contrast are *of* amounts or magnitude of elements or components. Proportion and direction bear on placement of elements or components.

CO-ORDINATING PRINCIPLES

Whereas the inherent relationships, when controlled, make their individual contribution to design, other principles when applied, co-ordinate these individual forces to achieve further objectives or attributes of good design.

The co-ordinating principles are dominance, balance, and rhythm.

Dominance is the greater force exerted by one or more of the elements.

Darwin and Mendel each discovered the importance of the law of dominance—one in evolution, the other in heredity.

Balance is equilibrium of visual attractions, weights, or forces around an imaginary central vertical axis.

Rhythm is eye movement induced by dominant directional forces.

We are indebted to Newton for the discovery of the physical laws that underlie both balance and rhythm. Balance is a concept of Newton's Law of Gravity; rhythm, a concept of his laws of inertia and motion.

SCOPE OF CO-ORDINATING PRINCIPLES

We are again faced with the two problems of magnitude and placement—this time as between and among all the principles.

The principle of dominance serves as a basic guide to "How much?" Dominance is the co-ordination of repetition, variation, and contrast, together with proportion—as proportion relates to amounts of chromatic elements.

The next question, regarding placement, brings up several other questions to be answered first.

Everything that exists on earth is either at rest or in motion. It is either static or dynamic. At rest is, normally, a single state of being. Motion, however, can be slow or fast, sustained or interrupted, rhythmic or jerky. We must decide how strong each of these forces should be and which shall have greatest importance in our design.

The principle of balance is the basic guide to achieve a state of rest. Balance, a static force, is the co-ordination of repetition, variation, contrast, and direction, with proportion—as proportion relates to placement of structural elements. This furnishes a guide to placement of *some* components.

The principle of rhythm is the basic guide to achieve a state of motion. Rhythm, a dynamic force, resulting from the co-ordination of repetition, variation, and contrast, with directional forces, furnishes a guide to placement of *other* components.

Dynamic Balance is the co-ordination of the opposing forces of balance and ryhthm.

THE MINOR PRINCIPLES

The minor principles are not as all-inclusive as the major principles. They are only partial in scope. They may apply to only some of the elements, or they may be but a facet of one or more major principles.

Some of the minor design principles are: scale, gradation, transition, and radiation. Each is discussed in connection with the major principle of which it is a facet.

INTERDEPENDENCE OF DESIGN PRINCIPLES

Repetition, variation, and contrast underlie all other design principles. All design principles are interdependent. Each principle furnishes a counterforce to one or more other principles.

Contrast sets up opposing forces to dominance and repetition. The latter builds up, strengthens, and augments the force of the greater elements. Contrast of the lesser elements counteracts them.

Balance, a state of rest, is opposed to rhythm and direction, a state of motion.

These are but examples of the interdependence and opposition of the principles. These are brought out further in the study of each principle.

COMPLEXITY OF RELATIONSHIP

What is simple when one principle is discussed in regard to two elements becomes complex when all principles and all elements of all components are considered in the ultimate design. Some aspects of this complexity may be observed in the relatively simple design on the right.

All the principles, inherent and applied:
    repetition, variation, contrast;
    proportion, direction;
    dominance, balance, rhythm;
must be considered in the relationship of all the elements, structural and chromatic:
    line, form, space, size;
    color, value, texture;
    pattern;

as between or among all the components:

1. each piece of plant material to each other and to all the plant material;

2. the plant material to each space created by it and to all the space;

3. each space to each other and to all the space;

4. the container to the plant material, the space, and to the whole arrangement;

5. the accessory, if any, to the plant material, space, container, and to the whole arrangement;

6. the plant material and container to the total space.

Each of these areas of relationship should be constantly kept in mind throughout all further study of the principles.

Complexity of Relationships. The following are some of the many relationships created in the relatively simple design on the right:

Repetition of color and texture, with variation of size and form of leaves.

Variation of pattern of leaves and spaces between groupings of leaves.

Repetition and variation of size, form, color, and texture of three tulips.

Repetition of color and texture and contrast of size and form of three tulips to fourth tulip.

Variation of color and texture and contrast of size and form between foliage and container.

Variation of color and texture of container to background spaces.

Variation of form and texture, with contrast of size and color between flowers and container.

Etc., etc.

Inherent Relationships. Repetition of hue, variation and contrast of value, contrast of form and texture, all in the plant material and container; contrast of hue and value of background—these were all present before the material was organized.

Repetition and Variation

INHERENT IN PLANT MATERIAL

Repetition, variation, and contrast are laws of universal order. They apply to all nature. We, as flower arrangers, are concerned with these relationships as found in plant material, containers, and other components. Repetition and/or variations and/or contrast are inherent in *all* plant material. The following are examples:

Most open blossoms on an apple tree have *repetition* of form, size, color and texture. The leaves have *variation* of size, form and of the spaces between them. The rounded flower form *contrasts* with the linear form of the stem; the velvety texture of the blossoms, with the coarse texture of the bark; the pink of the buds, with the green of the leaves.

On a gladiolus stalk there is *repetition* of size, form, and hue on the lower portion of the stem. On the next portion of the stem there is still repetition of hue, but *variation* in size, and in form—from the round open floret to the linear form of the emerging bud. Further up there is repetition of the linear form of the buds, with some variation in size, but marked variation in hue to green—as less and less of the petal is visible.

Beginning with repetition and through a number of small variations, we have reached the point where the first and last sizes, forms, and hues are almost in complete *contrast*.

All of the florets and buds on the gladiolus stalk are organized in an uncomplicated manner along the stem. In other material, the relationships may be much more complex.

INHERENT IN RANDOM GROUPING

Pick up any two pieces of material at random. Your second piece will be like, similar to, or different from the first; the third to the first and second, etc. This will be true as you continue to bring together any two and any additional components—whether flowers, containers, or backgrounds.

If you bring together several red roses and several pink larkspur, you have repetition of red hue and round form; light red value and linear form. You have contrast of round form and linear form, and variation of red hue and light red value. All of this is true while grouped at random, and remains true after it is placed in the container and regardless of how it is placed.

REPETITION

Repetition is the combining of like elements. Complete repetition is the combining of components having like form, size, color and texture, their only difference being their placement in space.

REPETITION IS BASIC

Although all principles are important, repetition is basic to all order or design. Repetition is orderly and the mind responds favorably to order. Repeated elements establish the core to which all other elements are related. Without repetition of any element all is chaos.

BOTH STIMULATING AND RESTFUL

Repetition attracts attention. When two elements are in the same visual frame, they stimulate more attraction than one element, six elements more than four elements, etc.

The more often an element is repeated, the greater is the combined impact. However, the importance of each individual element becomes less as the total becomes greater. Whenever foreground material repeats the color of the background as the iris do

Repetition and Variation of Form and Pattern. All the flower forms and the two leaf forms are basically alike. Variation in form and pattern is brought about by changing the angle from which they are viewed.

on page 173 that color becomes more important, but the individual foreground element becomes less important.

Having first attracted attention by sheer numbers, the eye becomes adjusted to this repetition, so it ceases to evoke further reaction.

TOO MUCH IS BAD

Since repetition is so basic and contributes so much to order and design we may be tempted to conclude that if some is good, more would be better. Such is not the case.

Too much repetition of the same element results in monotony. Too much repetition of a number of ele-ments can be redundant— the story is repeated too often. In many period arrangements and old-fashioned bouquets, we find too many things repeated too often. One dozen greenhouse roses, with repetition of form, size, color, and texture, twelve times over, when arranged pin-cushion fashion, with repetition of spaces between them, will be monotonous and uninteresting. Variation and contrast are needed to rearouse attention and interest. Note the repetition with variation and contrast on pages 71 and 173.

This bears out an observation already made while studying the elements. A dahlia or zinnia, because of repetition of petals, radiating lines, and concentric circles, is a strong "eye-stopper," but the eye soon tires. The iris, on the other hand, does not seize the attention as quickly, but holds it longer because it has repetition with variation.

VARIATION

Variation of two elements means basic similarity with minor differences.

Variation of two components means repetition of one or more elements with minor differences in others.

We can find a counterpart in horticulture where a variation is a plant basically like its parent, but with some modifications or differences.

The degrees of variation possible between exact repetition and contrast of two elements—combinations of some repetition and some difference—are many. In design we are concerned with the relationship of each element of every component, to each element of every other component, so what were many possible combinations now become an infinite number.

There is no sharp line between variation and contrast. In the design on page 125 it is difficult to draw the line between variation and contrast of form. When the likeness is greater than the difference the relationship is one of variation; when the difference is greater than the likeness, the effect is one of contrast.

VARIATION CREATES INTEREST

Variation stimulates and produces interest. Whereas repetition dulls, variation invites the eye to stop again and again to experience some new or added detail or modification. The arrangement on page 88 has repetition and variation of form and pattern. The one on page 174 has repetition and variation of form, pattern and color.

Variation in spaces created by plant material is just as important as in the plant material itself. Note that in the design on page 113 there is variation in the width and length of the spaces, just as there is variation in the linear forms.

Variation in regard to *more than two* elements may become gradation or transition.

GRADATION

Gradation is variation at regular intervals, in one direction or sequence. The snapdragon or delphinium that has buds, several stages of partly opened flowers, to fully opened flowers has gradation of form, size, and color.

The arrangement on page 90 has gradation of form, size, and space.

TRANSITION

Transition is variation or a series of variations from one element or component through one or more intermediate to an unlike element or component. In the arrangement on page 76 notice how the tulip leaves give transition from the linear branches to open tulip blossoms. On page 101 the curled gourd gives transition from the vertical lines to the circular base.

COLOR INTERVALS

Repetition of color intervals is the use of hues spaced equally apart on the hue circle, or of values or chromas spaced equidistant on a color chart. Variation of color intervals is the use of hues, values, and chromas spaced unequally.

Repetition is basic to all order or design; it establishes the core. Variation stimulates interest and gives substance thereto.

Gradation. A gradual change in size, form (both linear and contained) and space.
Geometric Style. Geometric pattern within a geometric form.

Contrast

Contrast is the bringing into close proximity two elements that are opposite or unlike.

Complete contrast is the bringing into close proximity two components, all of the elements of each component being opposite or unlike.

Contrast can be between elements of equal magnitude or between elements of unequal magnitude. When the elements are unequal, *the lesser is always referred to as the contrasting material.*

Contrast is strongest in immediate proximity. If some distance or another element intervenes, the effect of contrast is lessened. If several elements intervene, depending on what these elements are, contrast may be entirely absent. There can be contrast of every element: the curved line to the straight; the round form to the angular; the large space to the small one; the yellow stamen to the purple petals; the white flowers to the black vase, etc.

CONTRAST EXCITES

We have already found that too much repetition dulls the visual sense and results in monotony. Contrast re-excites the optical nerves and heightens our visual response. When there has been too much repetition of the same elements, use of one or more contrasting elements sustains interest and prevents monotony, as in the illustration on page 104.

CONTRAST EMPHASIZES DIFFERENCES

By bringing together opposites in close proximity we invite comparison and call attention to their difference. The illustration on page 86 employs strong contrast of forms and textures. It makes these differences appear to be greater than when these same elements are farther apart.

CONTRAST OF UNEQUALS

STRENGTHENS THE STRONG

Contrast between two opposite elements of unequal magnitude strengthens strong form, color or texture. Since all strength or weakness is relative and contrast emphasizes differences, combining a bold form with feathery material will generally make the bold form appear bolder. Using a strong color with a weak color makes the strong one appear even stronger.

WEAKENS THE WEAK

It follows from the above that, by comparison, weak material will seem even less important. A piece of asparagus fern will appear weaker when combined with an anthurium than if seen separately. In the design on page 123 the small leaf forms appear smaller in contrast to the large rhubarb leaves.

CALLS ATTENTION TO INDIVDUALS

Both strong and weak elements will attract more attention when contrasted than if combined with their own kind. The single fern will be weak along side the anthurium, but will still attract more attention than the same fern surrounded by others of its kind.

This is often the case when only *one* flower is used in an arrangement of foliage or other material. The flower is weak in relation to the other material but cannot be ignored because contrast emphasizes the difference between it and the rest of the arrangment and calls special attention to its weakness.

INTENSIFIES EQUALS

Contrast of equals intensifies both. When a triangular form is combined with a round one of equal size, the triangular form will seem more angular, and the round form, more compact. When bright red is combined with bright green of equal magnitude, both will appear more intense.

Since very smooth or shiny textures and very rough textures are both strong textures, equal areas of glass or silver and rough bark or coarse-textured flowers, such as hydrangeas, will emphasize both. Each will appear stronger and each will attract more attention than either used alone or with others of its own kind.

Equally strong elements divide attention, and contrast that strengthens both makes the division of attention more pronounced. Attention will constantly shift from one to the other. The result will be one of continued competition rather than harmony.

We have already observed that as the eye adjusts itself to light it adjusts itself to color intensity. When two components are of different hue, but equal in size, form and intensity, the eye will adjust to intensity within a short time and the colors will appear weaker; consequently the hues will appear of lesser contrast than at first.

DIFFERENCES ADD UP TO EQUAL

Problems of contrast are often far more involved than the above simple conclusions seems to indicate. Combine a large purple Jackman clematis with two or three bright orange blossoms of the trumpet vine. Here we have contrast of size, form, hue, and chroma, but the strong elements are not in the same component. Different elements of each flower are emphasized but neither component, taken as a whole, is stronger than the other. The impact of opposition will draw the eye and attention is directed to the difference. Whether this is desirable or not depends entirely on what the arranger is seeking to accomplish.

DISCORD

Contrast of several equals results in discord. When several unlike elements of equal magnitude are combined in close proximity, each will appear stronger than when used alone or with others of its own kind. Since the normal human mind focuses attention on one thing at a time, the attention, which before was divided, is now torn between a number of attention-getting forces and the result is discord.

Combine a white calla, a light blue cornfloweer, red salvia, a yellow sunflower, yellow-green hydrangea, violet-red phlox in an orange bowl and you have discord.

Too much contrast among all elements of all components results in confusion.

The problem becomes increasingly complex when each individual element and each combination of elements is considered in relation to every other element or combination of elements present in plant material, container, background areas and accessories.

CONTRIBUTION TO DESIGN

The contribution to design of good contrast is often unrecognized and its importance underestimated. *The more effectively contrast is used, whether bold or subtle, the less the viewer is aware of the contrasting forces.*

Not enough contrast is similar to too much repetition. It fails to stimulate attention and leaves the design insipid.

Creating a design can be compared to preparing an appetizing dish. Meats, vegetables, soups, and cakes are created of a combination of elements. Repetition and variation would apply to the ingredients used in greater amounts. These dishes would be flat and uninteresting without the use of other ingredients in lesser amounts. Contrast represents the application of seasoning. When a cake is delectable we say, "This cake is delicious." We never say, "This cake has just the right amount of salt," or "This salad has just the right amount of vinegar in the dressing." We are not aware *of the contrasting ingredients* — only the harmonious result.

Only when there is too much or too little do we react to the specific ingredient. If there is not enough salt in the soup, we almost automatically reach for the shaker. If you taste the garlic, there is too much of it.

So with our design. We react to the whole when the elements have been skillfully blended. Only when there is too much or too little contrast, does the element or absence thereof project itself into our consciousness. The student of design accepts what is good, but consciously rejects what is poor. If we were always consciously aware of good contrast, it would be easier to analyze.

EMOTIONAL RESPONSE

Set your dining table with your best china, silver, and crystal. Then place an arrangement of heavy pine, oak leaves, and fungus in a container of rough bark in the center. Here we have strong contrast of form, size, color, and texture. But the result is one that repels. Repelling is an emotional response based on past experience rather than a visual response. The emotional response, particularly in the realm of table setting, is one that cannot be ignored. The arranger and the judge must consider it along with visual response.

CONTRAST OF COLOR DEFINES FORM

In the previous pages we have discussed contrast of form, size, color or texture of components *in close proximity*. This included components seen separately and entirely, such as a larkspur and banana alongside of each other; partially overlapping components, such as a yellow rose among dark green foliage; and smaller components superimposed on larger ones, such as a green wisteria vine in front of a gray background.

When components overlap or are superimposed on larger areas, contrast serves an additional function.

When components are in successive planes, contrast of color, and in a lesser degree variation of color, defines form and space. Contrast may be of hue, value, or chroma.

It is difficult to distinguish a form placed in front of material having exactly the same hue, value, and chroma. This is particularly true when the light source is from the same direction as the viewer. When the light is from a different angle, shadows along the edges may have enough variation in value that form becomes recognizable.

The beautiful form of a pale yellow iris is not distinguishable in front of a pale yellow background. White is the strongest color. White petunias and moonvines can be seen after dark when all hues are gone. But all-white flowers in a white container against a white wall are "lost." Put the pale yellow iris or the white arrangement in front of a black or dark blue background and the entire form of the iris or the white arrangement will be clearly defined.

CONTRAST DEFINES WITH EMPHASIS

The greater the variation or contrast, the more readily an object or form is recognized.

The form of dark green foliage against a dark green background may be all but lost. The subtle variation of values in a dried arrangement against a brown background can be enjoyed only from a near vantage where these subtle variations make form recognizable. But the forms of white callas and their foliage contrasted against a red background are sufficiently emphasized that their impact is felt from a distance.

CONTRAST OF COLOR DEFINES SPACE

We have already recognized in our study of space that foreground lines and outlines of foreground forms outline space or background areas. It is the contrast between the two of hue, value, or chroma that delineates the foreground material, which, in turn, outlines space.

The white arrangement in the white container against the white wall failed to project not only the form of the arrangement but also the spaces created by it. The white arrangement in front of the blue wall on page 156 gave form to *both* the arrangement and to the spaces created by it.

Where color is the same, both form and space are indistinct. As variation of color increases, both form and space become more distinguishable. As contrast is reached, both form and space are clearly delineated.

WHAT COLOR BACKGROUNDS?

Generally gray or grayed hues are useful in background areas since these are weak colors that allow the plant material and container to exert the stronger force.

When the foreground is light and the background area dark, the eyes focus on the light areas. The dark background is beyond the focal plane or outside of the focal area. This creates a sense of depth.

When we place dark forms against a light background, the background will appear to come forward bringing all into the same visual plane. The result is a flat arrangement.

If the arranger's purpose is to create strong spatial areas and her foreground colors are weak or neutral, she may need to resort to placing strong color in the background and rely on size, form and texture to achieve foreground design interest.

A successful photograph is one that has strong value contrast between foreground and background material. If the subject and the background are too nearly alike in value, either one can be lightened or darkened by increasing or decreasing the amount of light directed on it. In either case form is defined by contrast of value. In an artists's sketch form and space are delineated by a black or contrasting line.

Neither device is available to us. It would be impractical for us to use light to lighten or darken any one area; nor can we outline shapes or forms with linear material. We do however, learn from nature. By placing some foliage — which is usually grayed dark green — behind flowers, we establish contrast of hue and value which define and emphasize the outlines of flowers.

To summarize:

1. Contrast excites.
2. It strengthens strong forms and weakens weak ones.
3. Contrast emphasizes differences.
4. Good contrast enhances design.
5. Contrast of equals divides attention.
6. Contrast of too many elements results in discord or confusion.
7. Not enough contrast leaves design insipid.
8. The wrong kind of contrast repels — an emotional response.
9. Contrast of color defines form and space.

We accept contrast that is good, without being aware of the contrasting forces. Only when there is too much or too little, do we react to it, or consciously reject it.

Scale

Scale is defined as:

1. Size of parts or components in any complex thing, compared with other like things.

2. Relative dimension, without difference in proportion of parts. (Webster)

SIZE COMPARISON

Scale is a minor principle because it applies only to the element of size.

Scale is repetition, variation, or contrast of size. Repetition is the use of sizes that are alike; variation, sizes that differ slightly; contrast, sizes that differ sharply. All of these are in good scale, or in scale. It is only when contrast of size is too great that components are in poor scale, or out of scale. Just as with contrast of other elements, close proximity intensifies size differences.

Scale is one relationship that can usually be determined before components are placed in the design.

Since size is inherent in all components and often actual size cannot be changed but only modified, establishing good size relationship is a greater problem in flower arranging than in arts where the size of forms is not predetermined.

In the design on page 97 there is *repetition* of size in the 10-inch hibiscus and the 10-inch container — but still the flowers were too large in comparison to the container! Why is this true? The flowers were too large in relation to the other smaller plant material; but all the plant material considered as a whole was too large for the container; or conversely, the container was too small for all the plant material. Neither

the flowers or container could be reduced in actual size. By turning the flowers to one side, and surrounding them with a *grouping* of leaves, they appeared smaller; by adding a wide base under the container, it appeared larger. This brought the large hibiscus and the container into better visual scale.

Size comparison may be expressed separately as scale, or it may be included with other elements while considering repetition, variation, and/or contrast.

FUNCTION AS RELATED TO SCALE

Man is conditioned to accept size as indicative of function. A 15-inch candle would appear in scale on a four-foot table with two place settings, but a 15-inch salt shaker would appear to be out of scale on the same table, even though both are essentially the same size in relation to the table. The 15-inch candle is functional, and might even be taller to serve its purpose better, but a 15-inch salt shaker is too tall to serve two people — or any number of people. Thus what is seemingly considered in terms of size as compared to other sizes in the same design, is actually considered in terms of function.

MINIATURES

Scale as defined in the second definition is important in miniatures. A miniature is a model of a larger design. This may be a miniature arrangement or a miniature scene. In these art forms, the sizes of all components are scaled down, i.e. a reduced scale is established according to a fixed ratio. The size relationship — not the size — should then be the same as for normal sized arrangements, life-sized landscapes, or other scenes. Having established a scale, individual parts are then either *in* scale or *out of* scale.

SCALE OF FIGURINES

The question of scale often arises in regard to figurines. This is because plant material is life-size while figurines are usually scaled down. A human figure may be reduced to various scales; a giraffe may be reduced considerably; a bird may be reduced very little. Such variation in scaling down is also true of figurines representing inanimate objects such as lanterns, windmills, etc.

Only when a scene is called for need the size relationship between the figurine and other material approximate life-size relationship.

Figurines used as design components, as on page 12 to contribute their share of form, color, and texture to an arrangement, are considered in terms of actual dimensions.

Since miniature arrangements are scaled down arrangements, not scaled down scenes, figurines in miniatures should be considered in terms of their contribution to the design.

SMALL ARRANGEMENTS

The small arrangement is not a scaled down arrangement nor a model of a larger one. Often the small arrangement is a part of a larger composition such as a coffee, card, or lamp table, etc., where it is viewed from above, where its height is not important, and where its size is determined by the number of other objects in the available space.

Solving Problems in Scale and Proportion. The 10-inch hibiscus blossoms and the individual pokeberries were out of scale—their contrast of size was too great. Turning the blossoms for a side view, and grouping of leaf forms in a concentric pattern around the blossoms, reduces their visual size in relation to the larger pattern. Grouping the recemes of berries causes the eye to see each group as a larger unit. They are now in better scale—there is now good contrast of size. The arrangement without the base was in poor proportion because of the narrow width of the container. Placing it on a wide base—thereby changing its lower width —without changing the height of the arrangement improved the proportion.

Proportion

Proportion is the relationship of the size or magnitude of one part to another or of one part to the whole. (Webster.)

Proportion in regard to structural elements is a relationship of:

1. The amount or extent of lengths, widths, thickness, area or volume of solids or spaces.

2. The placement of the above.

Proportion in regard to chromatic elements is a relationship of:

1. Color magnitude — area as modified by hue, value, chroma, and texture.

2. Color intervals.

Einstein has made us aware of the fact that everything in the universe is relative. Nothing is absolute. This is true of time, temperature, and *space*. All measurement is relative. Nothing is short, long, wide, or thin itself. It is only short, long, wide, or thin in relation to something else.

PROPORTION INHERENT IN COMPONENTS

Since form has dimension, the relationship of its length, width, and thickness, of its area or volume, constitutes its proportion. Consequently *every* form *has* proportion.

The length of an iris leaf, a castor-bean leaf, or a dahlia bloom may be the same, but the relationship of this length to the other dimensions varies from one to the other. The iris leaf is narrow, the castor-bean leaf is wide, and the dahlia is wide and thick. The difference between the narrow linear form, the wide two-dimensional shape, and a thick three-dimensional form is a matter of proportion.

Material on a living plant has proportion in relation to the rest of the stem or branch, and in relation to the entire plant. As you sever material from the plant, prune it, remove foliage, and change it in any way, you are changing its proportion. Its proportion while on the living plant, to the rest of the plant, is seldom of interest to the arranger. Once severed, its new proportion becomes important.

PROPORTION INHERENT IN RANDOM GROUPING

When you go into the garden and bring in a bunch of flowers, or perchance, make an old-fashioned bouquet out of them, the form of this bunch has proportion. If you carry a bucket of water in which to put your flowers, the form of the plant material has proportion, the bucket has it, and the form of the flowers and bucket together have proportion. If you go to the florist and he rolls your flowers within a paper cornucopia, this cone-shaped form has proportion. And any other bunching or random grouping has it.

PROPORTION MAY BE GOOD OR IT MAY BE POOR

Nature has given proportion to the form of the plant material. We change this proportion as we sever it from the plant. The artisan has determined the proportion of the form of the container. The architect, interior decorator, or the homemaker in the home, or the staging committee at the flower show have determined the proportion of the form of the space. Any one of these may be good or poor. It is our task to select or alter the proportions of the components and then reorganize them to create good proportion in the form of the ultimate design.

WHAT IS GOOD PROPORTION?

Good proportion is the *pleasing* variation of the dimension of one form or a part thereof to the whole. What constitutes good proportion, or a pleasing variation of dimensions?

Man has accepted as satisfying varying proportions to which he has been *conditioned*. There are two forces that have been active in conditioning man's acceptance: natural forms and man-made forms. Since natural forms — the shape of a leaf, a flower, or a tree, the contour of a sea shell, the silhouette of a bird or a butterfly at rest or in flight, and the human form — have remained more or less constant through the ages, man has been conditioned to accept their varying proportions and react favorably to them.

THE GOLDEN MEAN

Because proportion deals with dimensions, it is a principle than can be expressed in a mathematical ratio.

The constant ratio of numbers known as the golden mean, can be expressed numerically as follows: 2-3-5-8-13-21-34-55-89-144-233 etc., to infinity.

Note that any two adjacent numbers have approximately the same ratios, namely 1 to 1.6, and that this ratio remains the same no matter how far the numbers are extended. This is the ratio, regardless of dimensions, that we often find in nature.

Any two dimensions having this ratio are in good proportion.

Any three consecutive dimensions in such a series are in good proportion. In fact, any four consecutive dimensions can be used together in a pleasing arrangement of sizes.

In the classical Japanese arrangement this ratio is used to arrive at the height of the plant material in relation to the width or height of the container. Then, using this tallest or "heaven" line as a starting point the "man" and "earth" lines are determined by the same, but descending ratio.

It will also be noted that a rectangle that is 3 x 5 has the same proportion of one that is 55 x 89 or 89 x 144. This relationship is known as the golden **rectangle.**

This proportion is found as the basic proportion of the classic Greek architecture. Time has certainly proved its excellence.

Since man has become conditioned to these constant proportions based on natural formations, they have been found to be most satisfying to most people. The golden mean thus serves as a good *guide* for the beginner.

Although relative dimension is the basis of proportion, we do not need a ruler to determine whether two elements are in good proportion. Instead, our reaction gives us the answer. "The design is too wide thru the center!" "The container is too bulky! . . . too long on the left." "The tallest line is too short for the container; . . . too little! . . . too squat." etc. Almost anything that is "too" is in poor proportion.

RESPONSE TO MAN-MADE PROPORTION

Man has at various times become conditioned to other proportions. Every new fashion looks "too something or other," until we become accustomed to it. Once we have accepted the proportions of the new fashion then the old fashion looks "too something else." The bustle and hoop skirt of the 19th century, the Gibson girl of the early 20th, or the flapper of the twenties are all "too something else" today.

The same is true of other forms: the horseless carriage vs. the sleek new auto styles; the "slim Jim" greeting cards; the bungalow vs. the modern house. All these have been changes in man-made forms. What at one time was accepted as good proportion was later rejected, and vice-versa.

The same is true in flower arranging. The judge may find herself torn between what was recently accepted as good proportion and to what we are currently being conditioned. Certainly the trend has been toward greater ratios. The golden mean which can fit beautifully into the home decorating scheme may be too squat in a flower show. The golden mean is *only pleasing.* It is not startling, exciting, distinctive, or eyecatching — all qualities which catch and hold the attention of the viewer, as well as that of the judge. In the face of accelerated competition, we accept as good proportion what was formerly considered "too" — too tall, too thin, too bold, too chopped up, too sparse, too angular, etc.

A design that is two to three, or even four times the height of the container as the one on the right may be preferred to one only one and one-half times. Space created by crossing linear material, formerly considered too awkward, is now recognized for the strong force it exerts.

Classical Japanese design, while claiming to adhere to strict time-honored rules regarding length of linear material, currently gets around these rules very nicely by "not considering" the tips of material in its measurements. It "does not count the tips" when establishing the height of a design, but the eye of the viewer does so just the same.

EQUAL DIMENSIONS LACK AESTHETIC APPEAL

Geometric forms that have equal dimensions are usually monotonous. The arrangement that resembles a flat square, disc, or equilateral triangle, a solid cube, sphere, or pyramid, or a linear form with equal sides, such as a horizontal crescent, or unmodified parabolic, is seldom interesting or aesthetically satisfying.

FUNCTION EFFECTS PROPORTION

Function, in relation to the place an arrangement occupies, is another important factor determining good proportion.

Proportion. In the design on the right, the plant material is almost three times the height of the container reflecting modern trends toward greater ratios of plant material to container.

Texture. The variation of green on the sansevieria leaf and the variation of gray on the container give a heavily textured effect. even though both are quite smooth.

Transition. The lower leaf and the curled gourd give transition from the vertical line to the circular bases.

Proportion May Vary Considerably. and still be satisfying. The arrangement above has its greatest dimension horizontally. Such an arrangement would be suitable for a place where height is not desirable.

The design for the dining table will usually have its longest dimension horizontally, to remain below eye level. The mantel arrangement may extend downward, even below the lower edge of the container. This is also true of the suspended arrangement, such as the one on the right. The coffee table arrangment which is viewed from above may be within the outline of the container. An arrangement in a glass cylinder on a windowsill may be made to be seen through the container. It may be entirely within the container, but still have good proportion. Notice how the arrangements on page 101 and the one above differ in relative dimensions, yet both proportions are good.

There should be good proportion between patterned areas and plain ones. This is another way of saying that groups of smaller lines, forms, or areas of color should be well related to larger ones. This is

The Suspended Arrangement.

Proportion. Since most suspended arrangements are placed at or above eye level, its longest line may extend downward, even below the lower edge of the container, and still maintain good proportion.

Balance. In a suspended arrangement actual weight is automatically balanced around a vertical axis passing thru the point of support.

Rhythm. The dominant rhythm is carried by the wisteria vine extending from upper left to lower right, and augmented by the placement of the bold forms of the poppies and the downward force exerted by the wisteria blossoms.

The Chromatic Design is a harmony of secondary colors.

Contrast of Form. The form of the long leaf, and the forms of the pointed buds provide necessary contrast to the repetition of flower forms.

Line Direction. The force of the diagonal line is greater than that of any space created by it.

often carried out with pattern being supplied by the plant material and plain forms by the background.

PROPORTION OF SPACE

Proportion applies to space just as it does to form. We are concerned with the proportion of each space, and the whole space, and with their relationship to each other and to the whole. Are the spaces interesting or dull? Do they create an interesting pattern? Spaces with equal dimensions are apt to be monotonous. Variation in size and outline with some contrast creates a more interesting pattern.

PROPORTION OF COLOR

All aspects of proportion, as it relates to the structural elements, can in some degree, be applied to the chromatic elements.

Proportion should take into consideration the magnitude of color, which is determined by the area, hue, value, and intensity of color, as well as the intervals between colors.

The following formula for color proportion, just as the golden mean, can serve as a simple guide for the beginner:

Stimulating color in smallest amount,

Static color in larger amount,

Releasing color in largest amount.

This formula produces variation in amount of color and variation in force of color.

It should be noted that nature combines flowers, usually of stimulating color, with greens of static hue against a horizon of releasing colors — blues, gray-green and grayish purple.

The difficulty in analyzing good use of color stems from the fact that we *accept* good application of the principles and this acceptance is often passive or subjective. Only when proportion is poor do we react objectively. The same adverse "too" signifies poor color proportion: too bright, too gaudy, too red, too gay, too much, too dull, too flat, too weak, too harsh, etc. This is just the common way to express poor color proportion.

Again, much that was too dull or too harsh has become acceptable after we become conditioned to it. A friend had papered her dining room with huge red roses. When her son returned from the army, after years of being exposed only to drab olive, he was shocked. "Mother, what possessed you to plaster all those huge red roses all over the place?" A few days later he began to admire them. After a few weeks at home he was no longer conscious of these large areas of stimulating color.

PROPORTION OF TEXTURES

Proportion applies to the element of texture. The use of unequal amounts of texture is more satisfying than the use of equal amounts.

OTHER FACTORS

Although proportion is a relationship of dimensions of form and amounts of color, other factors do effect proportion. These are factors that *visually* change the size of form or the amount of color:

Stimulating colors and bold pattern make a form or area appear larger.

Greater density increases chroma, and greater apparent weight increases apparent size.

Material placed higher in the design always appears to be larger than that placed lower. Material projecting forward appears larger than that within the body of the design.

A vertical or diagonal line appears longer than the same horizontal one. In a container a 10" height appears greater than a 10" width. A broken line or a bisected one appears shorter than an unbroken one.

PROPORTION EVOLVES

If two elements or two components are not in good proportion, how can we improve it? It is possible to bring them into better relationship by changing either one. We must decide which one will remain "as is," and which will be changed.

When starting an arrangement, the question, whether expressed or implied, always is "Where do I start?" . . . "With what do I begin? with the space?

the container? or the flowers?" . . . "What do I select first and then use it as the first component or element to which all others must then be related?" The problem becomes progressively enlarged because a change of any one element or component will change the relationship of all the others.

Theoretically we should be able to start with any component or element and proceed to add all other components or elements in a pleasing proportion. In practice, however, it is necessary to start with what is fixed, or over which the arranger has least control, or what is in least supply, and work towards what is more flexible, or in greater supply. "What is fixed," may be determined in the show, by the class wording; in the home, by the purpose the arrangement is to serve. Usually this means the space the arrangement is to occupy.

In the flower show it will be related to the size, form, color, and texture of the specific area, under and behind, that the arrangement is to occupy, within the limitations set up by the class wording. Though the size and form of the background may be predetermined, the exhibitor often has the privilege to change the color and texture with an overlay of fabric.

Other things being equal, in the home it will relate to the size, form, color and texture of the furniture or surface on which it is to rest, and to the size, form, color and texture of the area immediately in back of the arrangement. In addition it should be related to the larger area that the eye encompasses at the same time as the arrangement, and to what this area contains.

In the home, surrounding objects, which by their nearness may become visual accessories, thereby altering proportion, may sometimes be moved. The size and form of tables is fixed, but the color and texture of dining tables may be changed by the table cloth.

An outstanding exception occurs when an arrangement is made for the sole purpose of being photographed. The proportion of the background to the design can be determined after the arrangement is completed, or even after the picture is taken. This can be done by the camera or by "cropping" after the picture is developed, as can be seen by studying the pictures in this book or any other book.

The size, form, color, and texture of containers are relatively fixed and predetermined. However, even these can be changed to meet the arranger's need. The container that has good proportion can be painted a different color. This may also change the texture. The addition of a base, plinth, or mat increases the size as in the arrangement on page 97. Bringing material over the edge of the container or over portions of it as in the arrangements on page 104 minimizes size. Both of these changes modify the proportion. Arrangers soon start "collecting" containers to increase their choice and to allow greater flexibility in their work.

The arranger's supply of plant material may appear varied and plentiful and, in truth, it comes in countless dimensions and proportions. All has predetermined size, form, color, and texture from which she must select or reject or which she may alter. By cutting away she can reduce the dimensions and change the proportion of the plant material, but there is little she can do to increase any dimension, except by grouping of individual units, or to change its color.

The proportions of the relatively fixed components establish the starting point around which other elements are related. The proportions of the fixed elements suggests or dictate the choice of the variable elements.

The proportion of the final form evolves as the individual forms are positioned in different areas within the structural framework. The placement of the primary line establishes the height of the plant material; other placements establish the width; and together they begin to determine the proportion of the plant material to the container. But the proportion of the design changes almost every time an additional piece of material is incorporated into the design. A primary line that seems to be in good proportion when first placed in the container, is suddenly too short as other material is added. A longer line may need to be substituted, or an additional longer line may need to be added—for the primary line has not only become shorter (relatively) but also weaker and must be strengthened.

Color proportion also evolves as the design progresses. The color magnitude of each component as it is incorporated in the design changes the color proportion of the whole.

Proportion is relative dimension of form and relative magnitude of color. It is inherent in all components, in any random grouping, and in the ultimate design.

Direction

Direction is relative position in space of an element in regard to:

1. Its starting point.
2. Other elements within a unit.

DIRECTION INHERENT IN ALL PHYSICAL COMPONENTS

Everything extends in some direction from its starting point. This may be up, down, forward, backward, diagonal, etc.

Since no two points or areas of a single component nor any two components can occupy the same space at the same time, the second point, area, or component must be in some direction from the first.

The spacing of leaves or flowers on a stem gives direction to each leaf or flower in relation to every other one. The arrowhead leaf may point upward from its union with its stem, or it may be at right angles, or it may droop downward. Each petal on the camelia is in some direction from every other petal, from the leaves, or from its stem. Each point on a wisteria vine is in some direction from every other point.

The horticulturist has always recognized inherent direction. The blue ribbon dahlia or narcissus should turn slightly upward, in relation to its stem. The rose should be held erect in the same vertical direction as the stem. The curved or angular stem is seldom considered a good specimen. The direction of growing plant material is determined by various growth factors into which we need not enter here.

Inherent direction is never good or poor in itself. But since it becomes a part of the ultimate design, it is good or poor in regard to the purpose it serves. It must be considered in terms of its force in relation to other forces in the design.

ALTERING DIRECTION IN COMPONENTS

We may find it necessary to alter direction of components before or after cutting. The following are some techniques that may be useful:

1. Depress growing stems into a horizontal position. Buds such as the marigold or iris that normally emerge vertically from its vertical stem, will continue to grow upward, thus changing the direction of the bud in relation to the stem.

2. Place stems at an angle while conditioning. The snapdragon and tulip, whose tips readily turn upward respond to this treatment.

3. Bend cut stems. The direction of many stems, even woody ones, can be changed by careful bending.

4. Roll leaves. Rolling a leaf while gently rubbing it, changes its direction. Even the straight leaf of the gladiolus can be changed to desired curves.

5. Prune away offending lines. Remove all lines that do not extend in the desired direction. Although this does not really change direction, relative direction is changed. Sometimes pruning away a heavy branch may allow the more desirable direction of a lesser branch to become dominant.

6. Wiring. When all else fails we can even resort to wiring. A weak stem on a flower that looks down, when we want it to look up, may need the additional directional support that only wiring (unobtrusive, of course) can give.

IN RANDOM GROUPING

Since no two pieces of plant material can occupy the same space at the same time, direction is inherent in any random grouping of two or more units, such as a bunch of flowers. Their position in a bucket as brought from the garden, may be haphazard—not planned or controlled—but each is still in some direction from the others.

FUNCTION OF MECHANICS

The sole function of mechanics is to control the direction of plant material.

FUNCTION OF DESIGN ELEMENTS

During our study of the functional aspects of the structural and chromatic elements, we learned that:

1. A linear form, by its structure, requires the eye to move along in the direction of its entire length to encompass all of it.

2. Two-dimensional shapes, since they neither hold the eye or lead it on, allow it to move freely in any direction through the design.

3. Three-dimensional forms attract and hold, arresting directional movement.

4. Stimulating colors attract and hold, also arresting directional movement.

5. Receding hues lead the eye in a direction beyond the dominant plane.

6. Static hues or grays allow the eye to rest, or allow other than chromatic elements to direct eye movement.

CONTINUOUS OR CONTINUED

Continuous direction is found in line material. Line material exerts a single direct continuous force with or without change in direction. Continued direction, on the other hand, is a path of visual stepping stones along which the eye travels—stepping stones of form and/or color. It is a glide-rest-glide-rest movement. Two forces are involved. The direction of the stem of a delphinium, whether straight or curved, is continuous. The direction of the blossoms along the stem, following the same direction as the stem, is a continued one.

REPETITION OF FORM

Repetition of forms in a linear pattern establishes a continued direction. The overall linear form of the pattern then has the same quality as that of a simple line. In the design on page 109 repetition of hibiscus blossoms establishes a continued direction.

Repetition of form, alone, does not establish a continued direction. The old-fashioned bouquet seldom lacked repetition, but it was random repetition. No visual stepping stone path was established for the eye to follow.

A gradual change in the size of forms—within a linear pattern—has the effect of a tapering line. A gradual change in form from rounded to linear, size remaining the same, has the same effect.

Pursuant to Newton's law which says that an object at rest tends to remain at rest and an object in motion tends to remain in motion, we now have two forces: the round forms that hold the eye and the linear forms that lead it on. If the rounded forms are small or weak enough and the overall linear form is strong enough, there will be directional eye movement. If the rounded forms are bold, or the linear pattern is poorly defined, directional movement will not be achieved.

There must be repetition of *more* than a second form to achieve continued direction. Since forms are places where the eye rests (even momentarily) and the spaces between are the paths over which the eye moves, the eye would only move back and forth between the two forms. There must be additional movement, between additional forms until inertia is overcome and motion continues.

VARIATION OF FORM

Since too much repetition causes monotony and variation sustains interest, a more interesting movement results if there is some variation in the forms as well as in the space intervals between them. Since the spaces between the forms are either other plant material, such as foliage, or background areas, their size and shape are as much a part of the directional movement as the foreground material.

An apple blossom branch is more interesting than a branch of pussy willow. There is variation in the form of the blossoms as well as variation in the spacing on the branch—here both repetition and variation exert forces—as compared to the regular alternate repetition of the pussy willow buds.

It is immaterial to the eye whether the forms are all attached to the same stem, as the apple blossoms, or whether they are individual flowers grouped in a linear form, such as a spray of cornflowers might be.

If flowers that are round in form are attached to a visible stem, this stem serves to strengthen the directional force moving from one form to another.

Two-dimensional shapes, particularly those of foliage give transition from rounded forms to linear forms, and vice-versa. They bridge the gap between bold round forms and strong linear forms. They also allow the eye to move in any direction in the design.

Lines that extend forward lead the eye out of the dominant plane. Overlapping of leaf forms suggest successive planes, and leads the eye back into the design. Large leaf forms turned with the edge forward or turned at such an angle that there is a change from full view to edge view lead the eye into the design. All of these are instrumental in creating directional eye movement.

Many components are neither pure line nor repetition and variation of form, but have the characteristics of both to combine directional forces of both.

A line that becomes thickened or has added weight or has projections on it as in the design on page 177 does not allow the eye to move without interruption nor does it provide the rest-glide-rest movement of directional spacing of small forms, but instead it slows movement at these points.

The smooth line allows the eye to slide along quickly and effortlessly; the rough or variable line slows it down.

Repetition of Form Establishes Continued Direction. Repetition of form, in a linear pattern, first of the caladium leaves, then of the hibiscus blossoms, establishes a continued direction. All are part of a strong rhythmic movement.

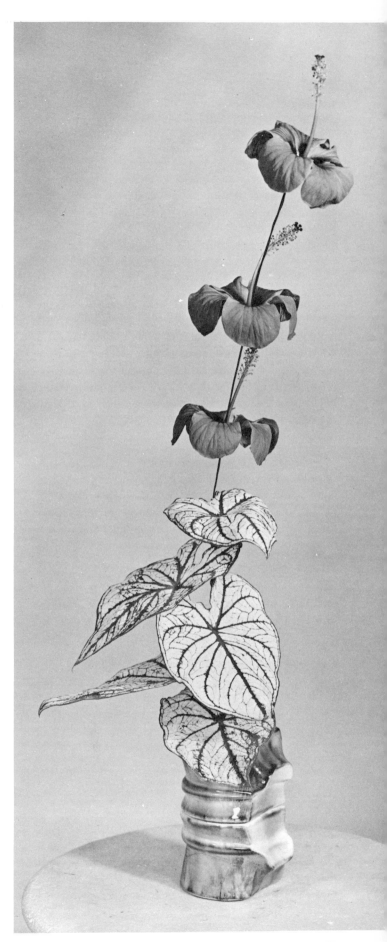

COLOR DIRECTION

Color direction may be a continuous flow of color, with or without a change in direction. Such continuous flow is similar to line direction.

Color direction may also be a visual stepping stone path of areas of color along which the eye travels. Just as repetition and repetition with variation of form within a linear pattern establish directional movement, so these two principles applied to the chromatic elements establish directional movement of color.

In each color dimension there are color direction possibilities: repetition of one hue, or variation from one hue to the next; repetition of any value, or variation from light to dark or from dark to light; repetition of intensity or variation from strong to weak, or from weak to strong. Color repetition or variation need not be confined to any one dimension, but may move through two or all three simultaneously.

An excellent example in nature of color variation through all three dimensions is an evening sunset: brilliant advancing hues in the sun itself, a gradual but varying change through dark values of red-orange, through hues to red-violet and finally blue, and through chromas to misty gray.

Mere repetition of chromatic elements does not establish a continued direction. There must be repetition in a linear pattern.

MORE THAN TWO COLORS FOR COLOR MOVEMENT

More than two areas of color are required to establish direction of color. If only two areas of color are used in a design, the eye would move back and forth between them. Three or more areas of color are needed for the eye to move onward in a given direction.

Since too much repetition causes monotony and variation sustains interest, a more interesting color movement may result if there is variation in the amount of color, the spaces between the colors, and in the color intervals.

We have outlined the directional forces of the structural and chromatic elements as separate and distinct forces—which they are. But since color never exists per se in floral design, but is always superimposed on form, we are always concerned with the combined directional impact of all elements.

In the component parts this is seldom a problem. In a single long leaf or stem, color usually remains constant or changes gradually, so color contributes to eye movement. So do forms on the same stem, since flowers or leaves usually have repetition or gradation of color. In these the color pattern follows the form pattern, and any linear direction established by the latter will be supplemented, rather than disturbed, by the former. However, when we combine a number of components, each introducing variation or contrast of form or color, establishing a directional movement may become a problem. In the restrained design the solution may be simple. But in the luxuriant design, in which many forms and colors are co-ordinated, the problem becomes complex.

FORCE OF DIRECTION

Just as the eye is forced to move further to encompass a linear form, so the directional force is greater in linear forms than in other elements. We can analyze directional forces in lines more readily and then conclude that similar but lesser forces exist in other elements.

Direction implies directness—an undeviating or straight course. Any other course is the result of a *change* of direction. The curved line has a *constantly* changing direction. The angular or zigzag line is a connected series of courses each having its own direction.

The iris leaf has a direct course. The curling bitter-sweet changes direction constantly. Each branch of the huckleberry is direct at a different angle. The branch of the apple tree or a spray of euonymus may combine all three types of direction.

ART vs SCIENCE

The artist speaks of forces and tensions created in a work of art. Mathematics and physics are the means by which we can determine and measure forces and tensions. Although the forces in art may be too weak or too subtle to be measured with instruments, nevertheless, they are subject to the same laws of physics.

The following *physical* concepts apply to forces in design just as they do in pure science. Understanding these forces will help us to control them:

1. A straight line has more force than a curved line.

2. The force of a large line is greater than that of a smaller one.

3. A line can lead the eye in either direction.

4. Two lines of equal size have equal force. If extending in opposite directions they will neutralize each other. Conversely, two converging lines have greater force than one alone.

5. Objects at rest tend to remain at rest; objects in motion tend to remain in motion.

Force of Line Direction. In the design on the right, lines extending in nearly the same direction, strengthen each other, and have the force of a larger line. Lines radiating outward lose force as they move away from each other—concentrate their forces as they converge.

Dominance. Lines are the dominant element, with the contained forms of the hemerocallis and the container being subordinate.

THE STRAIGHT LINE

The force of a straight line is direct and bold. The stiff straight line of the gladiolus leaf takes you there without dilly-dallying. If cut square across the top, it may stop so abruptly that it will give the viewer a visual jolt. A grouping of these will march on together. These are often useful in the geometric, modern, abstract or interpretive styles.

In our study of the elements we have already observed that force varies with size—the larger the line, the greater the force.

The path described by a linear form can be travelled in either direction. This is indeed fortunate, for if the eye could never return over the same path, every straight line would take the eye either out of the design or down into the container. Straight lines moving into the design should generally be stronger than those moving outward so that the eye is always brought back into the picture. Curved lines can bring the eye back into the picture without going back over the same route.

Two lines of equal size have equal force. If extending in opposite directions they will neutralize each other; if converging, will create a concentrated force that will carry the eye beyond the point of convergence. The tug-of-war exemplifies strong opposing forces that neutralize each other. The arrow that points is a good example of a concentrated force. At the point where the lines converge the force is increased so that it carries the eye beyond the point of convergence. The arrow is a functional form to direct the viewer far beyond and in the direction established by the meeting of the two forces.

The concentrated force of converging lines varies conversely with the angle between them; the smaller the angle, the greater the force. An illustration of this force is the old-fashioned hairpin or clothespin that stays neatly in place as long as its two sides are almost parallel —but when spread apart so that its two sides converge at one end, "pops out" in the direction of the convergence.

When we bring together several lines extending in nearly the same direction, we increase their forces by adding them together, as in the design on page 111. This is what occurs when we strengthen our primary line in a design with supporting material. The effect is similar to that of a single larger line. This is true whether the lines are straight as on page 111 or curved as on page 117. The intertwining wisteria vine in the latter illustrates both the physical and visual support that one line gives another.

When two lines extending in the same general direction are separated by space, the space created between them now becomes important. It acts as a separator but at the same time it creates tension between them. In the design on the right the spaces between the parallel linear forms are as important as the forms. If two lines are separated by a larger space, or by other components, other nearby material may completely remove any tension between them.

RADIATION vs CONVERGENCE

Radiation—lines extending out in several directions from one central point.

Convergence—lines coming together from several directions to one central point.

Radiation and convergence usually is repetition of lines or forms and repetition of spaces between the lines or forms.

It is obvious that radiation and convergence are two versions of the same linear pattern. Both deal with the same lines, but in opposite direction. The sunflower and the daisy are examples of two-dimensional material having radiation and convergence; the pine needle cluster and the yucca plant are examples of three-dimensional material.

Radiating lines lose force as they extend out and further apart. Tension between them becomes less. Converging lines concentrate their forces to create a strong holding force at the point of convergence. Convergence is the greater force involved, as in the design on page 111.

Tension of Space. The long narrow spaces between the parallel linear forms of the candles create tension between these. The narrower the space, the greater the tension; the wider the space, the less the tension.

Which term is used will depend on which force we are describing. Since lines in nature seem to converge at a distance, converging lines can be used to suggest depth in a design.

These forces in plant material are seldom as clear cut as the above analysis in regard to pure line may appear. Flower heads are not made up of pure line or line direction, but rather of linear forms with tapering ends of petals. The tapering end is the convergence of two outlines where a secondary force comes into play. Its force depends on the strength of the outline. The tubular and tapering ends of the cactus dahlia petals have greater radiating force than the thin even lines of the pine needles. In fact, they sometimes almost neutralize the forces of convergence at the center.

Radiation may be complete in all directions, such as is found in many flower heads, or it may be partial as in a fan or in plant material emerging from the container.

In the symmetrical radiating pattern all lines are of equal length and have equal angles between them (repetition of lines and spaces with gradation of direction.) This pattern is often used in a horizontal design which is viewed from above, or the semi-circular fan-shaped design. A static design is the result. There are times when we wish to accomplish just that—to hold the attention rather than force it to move about—so this may be the very device we would employ.

In the asymmetrical radiating pattern, as found in the leaf of the castor bean or Rex begonia, lines and angles are not equal. These hold greater interest since the forces of the lines do not neutralize each other; instead create tension between the longer lines and the force of convergence.

Two crossing lines may have the effect of converging lines or may have the effect of diametrically opposed forces—depending on the angle between the lines. When two lines come together at a narrow angle (automatically making the other two angles widespread), the resulting force is one of convergence. When two straight lines cross at right angles, there is a direct head-on impact of forces.

The differences between the above forces are similar to those in the following illustration. When two cars going in almost the same direction sideswipe, they meet with some force. When two cars collide at an intersec-

tion the impact is greater. But when two cars meet head-on, the impact can be completely shattering. This assumes cars of equal size. If, however, one is larger or is moving faster, it will inflict more force on the other car.

THE CURVED LINE

Whereas the straight line does not change direction, the curved line does. It may be a geometric curve with a constant or graduated change of direction or it may be a natural or flowing curve with variation in change of direction.

THE GEOMETRIC CURVE

The geometric curve is based on the line described by the circle, oval, spiral, cone, etc., or any part thereof. It represents a constant or graduated change of direction.

The line enclosing a circle or oval always brings the eye back to the point of beginning. It always encloses space. If the circle or loop is large, the linear aspect will be more important since the eye must travel some distance to encompass it. If the enclosed space is small, the effect will be similar to that of a small form.

The **crescent** is a geometric curved line. It is a part of a circle. When both ends of the crescent are equidistant from the point of support, it is a "lazy" crescent. Its force is similar to that of the clock's pendulum—too much repetition for interest. The point of support of the "lazy" crescent is unlike the point of the arrow. There is not enough convergence for accelerated force but only enough force left to carry the eye on to the other half of the arc.

If the arc is but a small portion of a circle, the eye will travel back and forth; however, if the arc is the greater portion of a circle, the eye will follow through and finish the circle. The "Loop-the-Loop" of the carnival midway demonstrates these forces. As long as the gondola swings back and forth the motion is similar to that of the pendulum or "lazy" crescent; once it covers more than half of the loop it is more likely to continue and complete the loop, rather than stop and return on the same side.

Halfway between the straight sided arrow converging to a point and the crescent with its constant change of direction, is the **parabolic curve** combining two straight sides with a curve between them. The parabolic curve is a segment of a cone parallel to one of its sides. It is an arc with two *equal* tangents. The angle between the sides may be wide or narrow; the sides may be long or short. The normal position of the parabolic arc, since it is a segment of a cone, is with both ends resting on a horizontal surface. Sometimes in table arrangements it is used in that position, with the curve on top and the sides pointing downward. In design, however, the two ends may point upward, sideways, or in any other direction.

The parabolic curve, being half-way between the arrow and the crescent, has some characteristics of both. The greatest force is in the direction of the convergence, but since convergence is not to a point, a small portion of the force of one side is carried along the curve to the second side where it becomes neutralized. As the sides of the parabolic arc are shortened and the curve between them becomes greater, it more nearly resembles one continuous line, rather than two converging lines, and takes on the charactertistics of the crescent. Many an exhibit, in a class calling for a crescent, has been scored down because the line was a parabolic curve—the ends pointing out, not in.

The force of the *form* of the parabola differs from its *linear* force, just as the force of a round form differs from that of a circle. The outline of the nose of a modern plane and the air currents created by it, is a parabolic curve; and so is the outline of the breast of a duck and the pattern it creates on the surface of the water. But the nose of the airplane and breast of the swimming duck are both *forms* with outlines that give least resistance to air and water in a *forward* direction just the same as the spread hairpin or clothes pin that "pops out."

The linear force of the parabolic curve—not the form having a parabolic outline on one side—varies with the length of the lines, the length of the arc, the angle between them, and their position in relation to the force of gravity.

A greater force can be established in the crescent or parabola by the simple process of shortening one of the sides. The crescent that is high on one side, shorter on the other has far more "swing" to it than the reclining crescent. Its length may be the same, but its position relative to gravity has been altered. However, when we shorten one of the straight sides of the parabolic curve—*it ceases to be a parabolic*—it becomes a line with a hook on the end. It has become a veritable crowbar and its force works on the same principle. The force of the long handle is transferred to the short end, resulting in a highly concentrated force.

The *shortened* parabolic is, indeed a step between the crescent and the spiral—the most forceful of all circular movements. We have been told of the force of a tornado or whirlpool, but few of us have experienced it. But if as a child you ever played "Crack the whip," and it befell you to be the "end man" you have experienced the force of a spiral. In fact the crack of a whip is the force applied to the handle carried along the linear path of the whip and concentrated in the tip. In the plant kingdom the spiral tendril exerts its forceful hold on the nearest object.

The **reverse curve** is sometimes a geometric curve. When both halves of a reverse curve are the arcs of a circle, the linear force is that of two crescents with a change of direction at the center. This change of direction acts as a brake. Eye movement slows down after the first crescent, but picks up speed again as it travels along the second arc.

NATURAL CURVES

Straight lines and geometric curves are limited in kind. Because they are limited in number, they can be catalogued as above. Natural curves are unlimited in number and have unlimited variation of direction. From the arranger's viewpoint some are good, some fair, some poor, but all are different.

The Hogarth curve is a reverse curve which need not be charaterized by the stiffness of the geometric. Hogarth was not thinking of geometry or of flower arranging when he espoused the "line of beauty." His *gently flowing* "line of beauty" referred to the line of a woman's back. Its flowing motion with its varied change of direction is the source of its continued charm.

The accelerated motion of such curves as the crescent or spiral is not present in most natural curves. Each variation in direction or variation in change of direction as on page 117 slows the eye movement so that natural curves have gentler movement.

There are almost no two curves in nature that are exactly alike. Each curve presents a new and interesting linear form to the viewer. When driftwood arrived on the scene amidst crescents, massed ovals, and tri-linear designs, a piece of driftwood was always a sure bet on a blue ribbon. Why? Each piece of driftwood had a different linear form that created interesting movement in any design that might otherwise have been but a stereotype of many previous exhibits.

The gently meandering movement of many natural forms allow the eye to move at a varied tempo—sometimes slow, sometimes faster, other times to linger—before moving on.

THE ZIGZAG LINE

The zigzag line is really a series of straight lines going off in random directions. This results in random linear forces. Some may neutralize each other; others act independently; while still other crossing lines result in convergence. The result is confusion. The huckleberry foliage, has a branching pattern that offers random size, length of line and random direction. It is generally useless in design unless heavily pruned so that the pattern of the remaining lines is one of co-ordinated movement.

The zigzag line *can* be a strong forceful line if one direction is dominant and the contrasting lines are minor ones. These are often found in the Euonymus alatus, sweet gum, or the rugged stems of an old mahonia bush.

THREE-DIMENSIONAL DIRECTION

The structural elements not only control vertical and horizontal eye movement in the major plane of the design, as set out above, but can be used to lead the eye back or forth through the design. They can be used to create actual and visual depth.

Since chromatic elements create stimulating and releasing forces, they can be used to implement the force of the structural elements.

Force of direction inherent in linear forms and in groups of linear forms is also inherent in other individual elements or grouping thereof, but in lesser degree. All these forces, whether strong or subtle, exist in any random grouping of material and must be controlled and so related to each other to achieve aesthetic design.

SPACE ESTABLISHED BY DIRECTION OF STRUCTURAL ELEMENTS

The size and form of space is created as the structural elements are being placed in the design.

Pruning, shortening, bending, etc., changes the direction of the structural elements of plant material. Placement of these in the design further modifies their inherent direction. The placement of one or more creates or changes the size and form of space.

In the four designs on pages 28 and 29 we have changed the size and form of almost every space by changing the direction of a single piece of plant material from the point of support.

Space may be completely enclosed by lines, or it may be only partially enclosed as in the arrangement on the right. Since the eye will continue in the direction that the physical lines have established, the partially enclosed space will still be defined space having size and form. One straight line cannot enclose space. A single curved line, however, because it changes direction, can outline areas. The curved line can come back on itself completely.

Crossing lines may enclose space also but the strong force of four converging lines or the impact of lines meeting at right angles is so great that the spaces created by them become secondary in importance. In the design on page 104 the force of the diagonal line is greater than that of any space created by it.

Natural curves in lines and outlines will establish free form spaces. The fewer and bolder the linear forms, the larger and bolder the spaces.

Linear forms and two-dimensional planes extending forward or backward, rather than laterally, establish three-dimensional space. Any curved forward or backward line or curved plane as on page 33 suggests a continuously changing direction beyond the actual line or plane to suggest spatial extent or spatial limits.

All other aspects of direction which are true in a two-dimensional plane are also true in three-dimensional space.

Natural Curves. Natural curves have variation of direction or variation in change of direction, which slows down directional movement.

Direction. The entwining lines support and strengthen each other, both physically and visually.

Inherent Direction. Direction inherent in plant material will carry over into the ultimate design.

EMOTIONAL ASPECTS OF DIRECTION

During our study of color we observed that in addition to a visual reaction there is emotional response, which is conditioned by the individual's and mankind's past experience. Similarly, in addition to the visual response, each direction evokes an emotional response which is associated with human experience.

The vertical direction, extending directly upward, is aspiring, dramatic, alert, poised, balanced, strong, soaring, severe, austere, inspirational and dignified. In the design on page 167 the strong upward line is soaring.

The horizontal, associated with all animate and inanimate things at rest, is restful, tranquil, passive, static, quiet, and calm.

The geometric curve, associated with precise and measured motion, is strong, dynamic, and modern.

The diagonal direction defies the law of gravity. It depicts motion. It is violent, dynamic, transitional, and active.

The zigzag line, going in several directions, depicts restlessness, indecision, and insecurity.

The Hogarth line, or other flowing line, is one of grace and beauty.

The drooping line depicts sadness and lack of vitality.

Crossing lines are forceful and aggressive.

Mixed lines are chaotic.

Direction is inherent in all components, in any random grouping, and in the ultimate design.

Direction, continued or continuous, as manifested in straight lines, geometric or natural curves, is the strongest dynamic force in design.

PART FOUR

CO-ORDINATING PRINCIPLES

DOMINANCE

BALANCE

RHYTHM

DYNAMIC BALANCE

Dominance

Dominance: The greater force exerted by one or more of the elements. Dominance implies the presence of subordination.

Dominance may be of size, line, form, space, hue, value, or texture; several of these; or all of these. Greater force or effectiveness results from the use of a greater amount or more interest commanding material.

Greater force implies something of lesser force. In order that a design may have dominance, a portion of the design must be subordinate. If there were no subordinate material, there would be no dominance because there would be nothing over which to dominate. In the arrangement on page 111 lines are the dominant element, with the contained forms of the hemerocallis and the container being subordinate. In the design on page 173 there is a dominance of light values in the flowers, with darker values of foliage being subordinate.

WHY DOMINANCE?

As a rule, we can concentrate on or enjoy only one thing at a time. If a number of activities or situations compete for our attention, we cannot grasp them all at once. Consequently a design should convey one distinct impression, instead of several competing ones.

DOMINANCE OF PLANT MATERIAL vs. CONTAINER AND SPACE

It is axiomatic that since we are concerned with design of plant material, the plant material should have dominance in relation to the container and the background. This is true in spite of the fact that the container and background, often being predetermined, suggest or dictate the structural or chromatic design of the plant material. They may furnish the "keynote" but must still play second fiddle.

The design elements of the container should be subordinate to those of the plant material. In the black and white photograph on page 135 the black container dominates the design. In the actual arrangement, however, the stimulating hue of the bright orange lilies was the strongest element in the design, with the container being secondary. The container should be visually smaller or of lesser strength than the total force of the plant material. On page 104 the force of the container has been reduced by the diagonal leaf.

What may appear to be an exception is the horizontal design totally within the confines of a flat container, or totally within a glass globe or cylinder. In reality, however, the container in these cases also serves as the frame or the limits of its space.

The container should be more subdued in color. This is not only important from the standpoint of color dominance, but also serves to establish better stability and balance. Intricate pattern of form or color of the container, or design or pictures on its surface will compete unduly with the plant material for attention.

The texture of the container should be subordinate. Shiny, bright containers, or other textures that attract attention to themselves, compete with flowers for dominance.

The background, or the space the design occupies should be subordinate. Since an arrangement exists in space and the size of the overall space must necessarily be larger than the arrangement, it might appear that the background would always dominate the arrangement. However, the space, with an arrangement in it, is no longer one large undivided space. The visible portion of the original space has been reduced and divided into smaller spaces by the plant material and container. If the color and texture of these spaces are subordinate, their total effect will be subordinate also.

An exception might be a decorative design. A design intended solely to enhance the area in which it is placed might consist of subordinate plant material used to create interesting background areas. Thus an arrangement of branches, foliage, or other material, linear in form and releasing in color, might serve to create an interesting pattern with the color and texture of the background being dominant.

Having accepted that the plant material should have dominance in relation to the container and background, how can we achieve dominance in the area of plant material itself?

DOMINANCE BY GOOD PROPORTION

Unequal sizes, amounts and/or force of elements are the first steps toward dominance. More of one kind of line than another, more of one form, one size, one color, or one texture, than of another, more forms of one color than of another, etc., all these lead to dominance. Good proportion of these unequal elements is essential to effective dominance.

DOMINANCE BY BOLD FORM OR STIMULATING COLOR

The use of bold form or stimulating color will help to produce dominance in design.

The linear form of the delphinium or of a piece of driftwood is bolder than most lines. The angel-wing begonia or castor bean leaf is bolder than most other leaves. In the design on page 123 dominance is achieved with the bold forms of the rhubarb leaves. The dahlia or lily is bolder than most other open or closed forms. These bolder forms are helpful in creating dominance.

A review of our study of the element of color reminds us that reds thru yellows are more stimulating than other hues; white and light values, more than other values; and intense chromas, more than other chromas. The use of these is helpful in creating dominance.

DOMINANCE BY REPETITION

An element used two or more times assumes greater importance than if used only once. Other things being equal, the element used a greater number of times will be more dominant than elements used less often. In the arrangement on the right not only is the bold leaf repeated, but its scalloped pattern is repeated in the container.

Five dogwood blossoms, with repetition of size, form, color, and texture, are more effective than one. Four lines of gladiolus foliage, with repetition of form, color and texture, are stronger than only one line. Two pink roses and three pink larkspur, with repetition of pink, give more dominance to pink than either used alone.

Repetition is helpful in creating dominance, but repetition alone does not always result in dominance. If repetition is scattered, it often serves to divide rather than strengthen a design. If each of five gladiolus leaves points in a different direction, the force of direction is stronger than the force of repetition, and this may be the very factor that prevents dominance. Repetition of weak material may not overcome the effectiveness of fewer bold forms or smaller areas of stimulating color. No amount of repetition of ivy leaves, in a design that contained one large orange Oriental poppy, would make the ivy the dominant element. This compares to the chorus and star in a play. A chorus will usually not outshine a dynamic leading lady.

DOMINANCE BY REPETITION AND VARIATION

Since complete repetition may become monotonous, the use of components which repeat one element and have variation of others, furnishes dominance with interest. On page 125 the pale pink of the magnolia blossoms is repeated, with variation in size and form.

DOMINANCE BY PLACEMENT

Attention can be drawn to or withdrawn from an element and its force increased or lessened by its placement in the design. Any element placed near the central axis, rather than to one side, assumes greater importance.

A component placed to the front or shown completely assumes greater importance than one placed in a middle or rear plane, or one only partially visible. A flower, leaf, or branch, brought forward will appear larger and more dominant than those further back. Plant material brought forward and over the edge of the container puts the container back of the frontal plane and minimizes it size. Both help to make the

Dominance of Bold Form. Dominance is achieved by use of bold forms, and by repetition of form and pattern in leaves and container.

container of secondary importance. The same flower, leaf, or branch extended backward from the center will appear smaller and less important. Such material partially hidden by overlapping foreground flowers or leaves, not only becomes still smaller, but may also be changed in form from round to linear or vice versa.

DOMINANCE BY GROUPING

By grouping we mean *repetition without intervening elements.* "United we stand, divided we fall," might well be a slogan for design elements.

Mechanics, such as a holder, which are required by the physical character of plant material often serve to bring material together at one point or in one area, thereby establishing a stronger area than if the same material were scattered.

GROUPING OF LINES

When three lines move in approximately the same direction, the nearer they are the stronger the resulting unit. Lines close together strengthen each other. Several lines close together as in the illustration on page 111 give a stronger linear movement than the same number of lines scattered throughout the design.

Since long lines create long directional paths, the longer the lines, the more important it is that several lines support each other—at least through such areas of the design where there are other competing forces. Physically, long lines need more support than short lines, so it is not surprising that our visual reaction is the same.

GROUPING OF FORMS

Forms, individually too unimportant to be effective in a design, can become the dominant element by grouping as may be seen in the design on page 165. This, again, is repetition within a limited area. Mere repetition is not enough, for if the forms are spaced too far apart, the tension that holds them together as a unit is weakened; consequently their force in the design is lost. For example, the hydrangea and lilac are natural groupings of small forms. If their individual florets were two or three inches apart, their force would be negligible.

GROUPING OF COLOR

Any color scattered about in small amounts results in a hit-and-miss pattern. The same amount of color, or even less color, when grouped, can become the dominant force. This is a technique employed by the landscape architect. He usually advises that plants should be in groups or clumps rather than set out individually.

COLOR TO SUPPORT STRUCTURE

Dominance in the color design should support the structural design. This is no problem as long as the bold forms and stimulating colors are confined to the same components. However, if the dominance in the color design does not follow the same pattern as in the structural design, dominance may not be achieved, as in the design on page 129, and in the following examples:

Five carnations can be the dominant factor through repetition of size and form. However, if each is a different color—white, red, yellow, pink and candy-striped—the dominance established with the structural elements of size and form is destroyed by too much contrast of color. The color design should do one of two things:

1. Repeat the dominant color in the dominant form. This augments or strengthens the dominant structural element.

2. Repeat moderate color in the dominant form. This does not strengthen the dominant structural elements, but, at the same time, does not weaken them.

Dominant color in subordinate size and form sets up opposing forces. Greyed-blue iris (bold size and form, subdued color) and sprays of white spirea (subordinate size and form, stimulating color), so often combined in springtime, fosters competition between the two areas and dominance is lost.

DOMINANCE OF TEXTURES

Use more of one texture than of another. Strong textures— whether the very smooth or the very rough— can be used to reinforce colors or forms that do not exert enough force in themselves. Since texture is more subtle than form or color, strong texture does not compete for dominance with strong color or form in another area, but is more likely to create secondary interest areas.

Dominance by Repetition of Form of flowers, with variation to maintain interest. Note that repetition of leaf forms is changed to variation by changing their direction.

DOMINANCE BY USE OF CONTRAST

Contrast accentuates differences. It heightens the impact of difference by calling attention to it. Since contrasting material is always the lesser, it will make the greater material appear stronger. An arrangement of a dozen red carnations, may lack dominance, even though the form is bold and the color stimulating. The addition of a generous amount of green foliage—contrast of size, form, color, and texture — will establish dominance in the red carnations.

A design of all white flowers in a white container against a white background lacks dominance. Place the white design against a dark red, blue, or black background, which furnishes a contrast of value, to create dominance in the white arrangement.

DOMINANCE OF CONTRASTING MATERIAL

If the bold form, stimulating color, and strong pattern are in the lesser material, it may become the dominant material as in the arrangement on page 180. Although there is very strong rhythmic force in the linear pattern of the foliage, dominance is in the lilies with their large size, advancing color, and converging pattern.

DOMINANCE IN RELATION TO ACCESSORIES

An accessory should be related to other components through its structural and chromatic elements and may be related through the idea or theme it is intended to express.

We react more compulsively to a living organism, or something that stimulates a living organism, than to inanimate plant material. So it follows that a figurine will be more dominant than plant material having the same color and texture and covering approximately the same area. The figurine on page 165 dominates the plant material although the latter is of greater amount.

Thus the use of a figurine may give rise to a problem of dominance. Plant material is life-size. Figurines may be life-size, but usually are scaled down versions of larger living beings, so have the impact of something larger and more important than the size of the figurine would indicate.

When we combine the inherent dominance of a figurine with that of placement by placing it in center front, it often becomes too dominant, and almost moves

out of the design. Placing some plant material partially in front of it, which moves it out of the frontal plane, may remedy this fault.

Frequently an arranger tries to balance too much plant material on one side with an accessory on the other. This may be successful if the accessory is subordinate. However, a figurine of a little girl wearing a bright yellow dress (combining two dominant factors) may overbalance the plant material on the other side and may be strong enough to dominate the whole arrangement. This, in itself, is neither good nor poor, but the result must be considered by the arranger in relation to what she is trying to accomplish.

If the arranger's intent is to keep the figurine subordinate, she must reassess the force and interest of the size, form, color, and texture of all other material in relation to the figurine.

Another problem with the use of a figurine or similar accessory is the fact that its size is not reduced as readily as that of plant material so that it remains dominant even though we hope to use it for subordinate interest. Its contrasting elements may be so strong that it no longer serves as a contrast to plant material, but assumes the dominant role. Again this is neither good nor poor in itself, but is a result that the arranger must recognize and respect.

There is seldom a problem of diversity or lack of unity in the use of plant material alone, but the introduction of an accessory often creates this problem. If the accessory that carries the theme or idea is not also related through its design elements, the diversity between the accessory and the rest of the components may be so great that the design will lack unity and "fall apart."

DISCORD

Although repetition of bold and stimulating elements can be used to establish dominance in design, their use can also bring about discord.

Repetition of several different bold forms, and/or stimulating colors will set up strong opposing forces. The mind is distracted among equally strong forces, and the result is discord. Combine a red anthurium with a large red zinnia, or put a group of bright yellow roses in one half and bright red roses in the other half of a design, or combine all four, and you have discord.

DOMINANCE IMPLIES SUBORDINATION

Having determined what principles and other factors achieve dominance, let us consider how to provide subordinate interest.

Subordination can be supplied by variation, contrast, or both. Variation alone is the use of similar but weaker elements. This furnishes subordination, but may not furnish subordinate interest. Subordinate interest may be provided by components that have variation of some elements, from the dominant ones, and contrast of others, or by components having contrast of all elements.

When contrasting material is of equal magnitude, it is advisable to make one or the other subordinate. One material can be reduced in effectiveness by appying the *opposite* means by which dominance can be achieved.

Another means is to integrate one or the other with its background. Strong contrast between foreground and background delineates and emphasizes that which is contrasted. On the other hand, lack of contrast of hue, value, texture, and pattern merges such material into the background, so that its forms and the spaces created by these forms are weaker.

In the two arrangements on pages 130 and 131 the foliage is of equal strength as the flowers, when placed in front of a gray background. The use of a green background weakens the green and strengthens or accents the violet. With the violet background the lilacs are weakened and the green foliage becomes dominant.

Dominant interest with subordinate interest is conducive to good design.

Problems in Establishing Dominance. The dominance of the figure possessing bold form, stimulating hue and value, and living significance, is challenged by the strong chroma in flowers and foliage—both intensified by the contrasting background—and by the repetition of strong highlights in every leaf.

Subordination by Repetition of Background Color. The green background lessens the effectiveness of the green in the arrangement. By contrast it heightens the effctiveness of violet.

The violet background lessens the effectiveness of the violet in the arrangement. By contrast it heightens the effectiveness of green.

Balance

Balance is equilibrium; a state of equipoise, between weights, different elements, or opposing forces. (Webster.)

In floral design we are concerned with achieving equilibrium by means of any or all of these factors. It is not surprising then, that an analysis of the relationship of these factors reveals that balance has many facets. Balance of visual weight or of different elements is covered in the following discussion. Balance of opposing forces is discussed under Dynamic Balance.

BALANCE OF STRUCTURAL ELEMENTS

Gravity is one of the natural forces to which all matter is subject. We may be living in a space age but most of us are still earthbound and so must be concerned with gravity, weight, and balance.

Weight is the manifestation of the force—the downward pull—of gravity. All physical matter has weight—the single force of gravity acts on all earthly matter at all times.

In physical balance an object must be supported from below, from above, or be counterbalanced, or it will fall to the earth.

Physical balance insures stability. Physical balance does not necessarily insure visual balance. It does however prevent the possibility of the arrangement falling on its face just as the guests or the judges arrive!

Since we are constantly subject to the force of gravity, we respond not only to the physical experience but we are conditioned to respond to the force of gravity as a visual experience.

Floral design is a visual experience to the observer. The arranger must be concerned with the effect of visual forces to establish a sense of equilibrium and visual comfort in the mind of the observer.

There are other kinds of balance besides visual balance, such as balance of power, balance of accounts, etc., where equilibrium is not related to the force of gravity; but in all cases where the visual factor enters, balance is related directly or indirectly to the force of gravity.

Trees, shrubs, and plants, unless influenced by other outside forces, such as storms, tend to have natural balanced development and growth. As we sever material from a growing plant, its future state of balance depends on its placement. Unlike proportion, which is always inherent, balance may happen to be present in random grouping, but must be planned and co-ordinated in design.

Balance is one of the answers to the question of placement. It is the guide to placement of elements in relation to gravity to achieve a state of rest.

DIRECT SUPPORT vs. COUNTERBALANCE

The simplest aspect of equilibrium is that of objects resting on a broad base. This is direct support from below.

This type of equilibrium is found in horizontal designs where material is "at rest." Here balance is no problem. Most fruit and vegetable arrangements fall in this category. However, the principles of proportion, dominance, and rhythm become more important.

Counterbalance must be provided where material does not rest directly but extends beyond the point of support. In this case it must be balanced with an equal force in the opposite direction in order to maintain equilibrium. Most floral designs fall in this category. The arrangement on page 135 depicts counterbalance.

In counterbalance, the force of gravity varies directly with the size of a form and its distance from the point of support. A small form at a greater distance is balanced by a large form at a lesser distance.

SYMMETRICAL BALANCE

Symmetrical balance is the approximate reverse repetition of elements at equal distance from the imaginary axis passing through the center of a symmetrical container. It is simple in its execution.

It does not matter what is used, or how much, as long as there is reverse repetition at equal distance from the axis. The result will be balance. The size and shape of the container have no bearing on balance as long as it also presents reverse repetition.

In a free standing design, reverse repetition should also be established from front to back, so that the design will also be symmetrical if viewed from one end.

The symmetrical arrangement is usually a static arrangement. Symmetry itself is neither good nor poor. Depending on dominance, it can be restful or disturbing; depending on proportion, it can be spreading, stocky, or stately.

Since there is equal quantity of material, as well as interest on either side of the central axis, the attention of the viewer may be divided between two areas of equal attraction, if bold forms or strong rhythmic movements call for simultaneous eye movement in two separate areas. On the other hand, if the boldest forms or strongest movement is over the central axis, constituting one area of interest instead of two equal but separate areas, the arrangement can be restful. If poorly proportioned the symmetrical arrangement can indeed be uninteresting, but if well proportioned, it may assume an air of stately dignity and repose.

ASYMMETRICAL BALANCE

A symmetrical design always has symmetrical balance, but it does not follow that an asymmetrical or unsymmetrical design always has asymmetrical balance.

Asymmetrical balance is that of approximately equal visual weight composed of different elements on either side of an imaginary vertical axis through the dominant plane of the design. Examples are on pages 117 and 143. These elements have different visual weights and are placed at different distances from the central axis, with no two individual elements in balance with each other.

Asymmetrical balance poses two questions:

1. Where is this imaginary vertical axis about which material is to be placed?

2. How can different elements be brought into balance?

Where is the vertical axis in a tall asymmetrical container? . . . in a flat container? Does it pass through the center of the container? . . . the center of the base? . . . the point where the material emerges from the container? . . . the highest tip of the plant material? Is it nearer the front or back of the container? Is it stationary or movable?

The problem of the arranger is unlike that of the painter, whose canvas hangs on a vertical wall within a definite frame and within a single plane, which can be divided equally down the center. It is more nearly related to the problem of the sculptor who deals with weight resting on a horizontal plane.

THE VERTICAL AXIS

The container may be dominantly vertical or horizontal; it may be symmetrical or asymmetrical.

The imaginary vertical axis may pass through the point where material emerges from the container, through the center of the container, or through the center of the base. Or it may pass anywhere within a horizontal triangle established by these three points.

This permits considerable leeway in the placement of the axis within the horizontal container *within certain limits determined by the arranger:* first by the choice of container or base, and secondly by the placement of the holder.

Note that in a tall symmetrical container, the point where the plant material emerges from the container, the center of the container, and the center of the base, are *superimposed upon each other,* so that the form of the symmetrical container imposes a fixed and immovable axis.

Counterbalance of Equals. Counterbalance of similar elements on either side of a vertical axis; also balance of spaces.

Dominance: In the black and white photograph the black form of the container is the dominant element. In the arrangement itself, however, the strong chroma of the orange lilies was dominant. The green foliage and the black container strengthened the force of the orange hue by contrast.

Because of the movable nature of the axis in the asymmetrical design, there are other factors that effect balance:

1. The longer or wider the container or base, the easier it is to establish balance. The wide container in the design on page 143 is an important factor in establishing balance.

2. The design that has actual or visual depth, or one in which there is a feeling of more than one vertical plane, will appear to have better stability than the flat design which lacks depth—just as a tricycle stands up easier than a bicycle.

3. The addition of an accessory to either side of the container visually widens the base. Since the addition of an accessory also adds weight to its side, both effects must be considered in relation to balance.

4. If there is a sharp line of division between the plant material and container, the eye seeks balance in the plant material itself, as well as in the design as a whole.

5. Conversely, some plant material over the edge of the container unifies the plant material and container, so that the eye reacts to the whole design.

VISUAL WEIGHT VARIES WITH ELEMENTS

Elements vary as to visual weight. The following appear heavier:

Denser and bolder forms—including greater substance.

Larger sizes—including greater thickness.

Darker colors—both hues and values.

Coarser texture.

You will note that greater substance is another aspect of size. It is greater size in the third dimension. Darker values and coarser textures may also be two aspects of the same thing. The shadows in coarse textures add dark gray so that colors will appear darker.

In regard to the structural elements of size and form, the opposites—smaller sizes and sparser forms—appear lighter in weight. As to the chromatic elements, it is not the opposites, but the middle ranges—the grayed colors and intermediate textures—that appear lighter in weight.

The opposite of the dark colors and coarser textures are the stimulating white and light values, and the other strong textures—the very smooth and shiny ones. Their effect on balance is further discussed under Balance of Chromatic Elements.

VISUAL WEIGHT VARIES WITH PLACEMENT

The apparent weight of an element becomes greater the further it is from the point of support and becomes less the nearer its point of support. This holds true not only for horizontal distance in establishing counterbalance, but also for vertical distance. Any form used high will appear heavier than the same form used just above the container.

Weight placed low helps to establish stability. Since it approximates direct support rather than counterbalance, it adds to the horizontal feeling. It makes the arrangement appear to be at rest. Too much weight placed low or "bottom heaviness" is often true of fruit and vegetable arrangements where actual weight may dictate placement of elements.

Since space has less visual weight than positive forms, some space under the base, the container, or portions of the plant material will reduce the feeling of too much low weight.

Visually heavy elements present in the container, since the container is the lowest component in the design, do even more to increase stability than those in plant material.

The effect of weight placed low and the resulting stability may be exactly what the arranger needs to carry out her theme; on the other hand, it may be a disturbing factor which the arranger should recognize and know how to handle should she want to create the opposite effect.

Material placed on or near the central axis need not be counterbalanced. Large sizes, bold forms, stimulating colors, or strong textures, which might be difficult to balance, if placed on either side, can be placed near the imaginary axis where their visual weight need not be compensated for elsewhere in the design.

COUNTERBALANCE OF UNEQUAL ELEMENTS

Visual weight, modified by the distance from the point of support, determines the force exerted in the given direction. A heavy element can thus be balanced by more of other elements that appear lighter if equidistant from the point of support; on the other hand, a heavy weight near the axis will be balanced by a lighter weight further away. A longer line balances several shorter ones as in the design on page 138. As with forms, a vertical line need not be counterbalanced, but diagonal and horizontal lines require compensating lines.

The important consideration in asymmetrical balance is the fact that no two individual elements balance each other. The placement of a single leaf creates unbalance with its inherent tension. The placement of a flower on the other side for counterbalance corrects the first unbalance, but since it is not exactly equal, creates a second unbalance, and a second tension, and so on. The sum total of visual weight on either side may be equal, but there are numerous unbalances between elements which create tensions and, consequently, eye movement throughout the design. It is this factor that makes asymmetrical designs more alive and interesting than symmetrical ones.

SUSPENDED BALANCE

In a mobile or other suspended arrangement physical balance is automatic. The axis always passes thru the point of support, and the force of gravity always distributes physical weight equally on all sides of this axis. This may or may not result in visual balance. If not, it is then necessary to change actual weight by using other components, or by increasing or decreasing their distance from the axis, so that physical balance will coincide with visual balance.

The mobile that does not have visual balance appears to *hang;* the one that has visual balance will appear to *float.*

Asymmetrical balance can lend interest to a suspended arrangement, as on page 103, or to a mobile just as it can to a stationary design.

Some mobiles carry the concept of asymmetrical balance to the nth degree by precise mathematical and scientific calculations: one unit at a greater distance from the central axis is balanced by a *grouping* of units at a lesser distance; in this group, a single unit is again balanced by a grouping of units, in which this progressive pattern is again repeated, etc.

SYMMETRY plus ASYMMETRY

The effect of symmetry and asymmetry are often combined in an arrangement. The container and the components outlining the design are in reverse repetition, but within the overall symmetrical form, there is an asymmetrical pattern of elements. Thus the tension that results from unbalance is often used to create a forceful design out of one that might otherwise be static.

Another version of asymmetry within symmetry exists in a pair of arrangements where one is the reverse of the other. Each arrangement may have asymmetrical balance but together they create symmetry; or each arrangement may even have definite and unresolved unbalance, but together they will establish a symmetrical unit. Such a pair would be suitable on an altar, a mantel, or buffet; or each can be individually supported, as long as they are near enough to serve as one decorative unit.

BALANCE vs. PROPORTION

In the pair of asymmetrical or unbalanced arrangements suggested above, whether the longer or heavier side is outward or inward has no bearing on balance. Which side should be longer or heavier will depend on proportion—the proportion of the forms or spaces between the two, or on either side of them.

Placing an arrangement at one end of a mantel, table, or similar surface, and a figurine or other accessory at the other end is often referred to as "balance by placement." If the arrangement and accessory were of equal size or interest, these equal but opposing forces would result in lack of dominance. What is usually meant is that a larger arrangement near the center will be counterbalanced by a smaller accessory at a greater distance. However this is not counterbalance since the two units do not rest on a single point of support. Instead, each is supported directly from below on a broad base, so that balance is of minor consideration.

Counterbalance of Different Element. One long dynamic upward sweeping line and the large space it encloses balances the several shorter lines and smaller spaces. The vertical lines do not require counterbalance.

Proportion is again the principle to be considered. The two—the arrangement and accessary—must be in good proportion to each other and to the three spaces into which the two units have divided the space.

Another popular misconception in regard to balance, is that the upper part of a design should balance the lower portion. Since balance is always related to a vertical axis in any visual experience, the relationship of the upper and lower portion is not balance, but proportion. A design that is top-heavy or bottom-heavy may still be in perfect balance, but lacks good proportion.

BALANCE OF CHROMATIC ELEMENTS

Let us review the forces that colors exert which determine their function in design. Stimulating colors attract. These are the warm hues, white and light values, and bright chromas. Releasing colors do not attract. Blues appear to recede. Dark colors appear to be heavier. These are the violet hues, lower values and black. Static hues and grayed colors are passive.

We are now concerned with the force of color in relation to each other and to their placement in design.

Since dark colors appear heavier, this is one characteristic of color which modifies visual weight of structural elements, so has already been covered in an earlier section of this chapter. The other three characteristics of color do not modify visual weight, but exert separate forces extending through the design.

STIMULATING COLORS

The force of stimulating colors is forward toward the viewer. When placed across or near the central axis, they attract the eye to the central axis without disturbing visual balance. However, too much stimulating color placed in front of the central axis has the effect of pulling the design forward.

With some stimulating color placed partially behind static foliage, the force of attraction is distributed between the planes of the design. The effect of color variation of overlapping planes is also a device for creating depth in design, since the force of attraction is carried through the design from front to back.

BALANCE OF SPACE

Space, although a visual element in design, contributes less to balance than foreground forms. The visual weight of space varies with different factors, one being enclosure. Open space appears to have less weight than closed space; closed space, less weight than foreground forms. Space does not balance solids. If space would equal solids in visual weight, then the sum total of solids and spaces on one side of a line drawn through the center would *always* equal the solids and spaces on the other side. Balance would never be a problem.

If all the releasing colors are placed in the front and all stimulating color in the rear, the stimulating colors will appear to be pushing forward past the releasing colors. To create this feeling place an arrangement of dried grasses and leaves against a bright yellow satin background.

Stimulating color used on both sides, but away from the central axis, will appear to make both sides come forward and away from the center of the design.

Since white and light values increase the apparent size of a component, they create the illusion of a stimulating force of a greater amount of color.

STIMULATING vs. RELEASING COLOR

Stimulating color placed to *one side* of the central axis, will bring that side forward, even though there is balance of visual weights. Releasing color on the opposite side of the central axis, regardless of the amount, will not neutralize this forward attraction, or balance the stimulating color. Receding blues, in fact, will lead the eye back into the design. Releasing colors *do not* serve as balancing forces to the stimulating colors.

A simple experiment will verify the above statement. Construct a foliage arrangement with good visual balance. Group three bright yellow chrysanthemums in a line crossing the central axis. Balance will be maintained. Now move these same three bright yellow chrysanthemums over to the far right side. The right side will now definitely appear to come forward. Neither the green on the left, nor any additional green that might be added on the left, will neutralize or balance the forward attraction of the stimulating yellow. If blues are used, instead of green, in attempt to balance the stimulating color in the design suggested above, the dominant plane, which is parallel to the viewer, will appear even more distorted.

A popular misconception in regard to color balance is that a small amount of intense color balances a larger area of diluted color, or vice versa.

If a design suffers from too much grayed brown, i.e., diluted brown, adding some intense yellow will not result in color balance, whether intersecting the axis or placed to one side. If anything, it will only make the color balance worse. Try this with any other hue, the result is invariably the same.

If a design suffers from too much green, and the addition of a small amount of red improves the color harmony, it is because we are supplying necessary contrast, not supplying color balance.

This does not contradict the statement that a small amount of intense color and a larger amount of diluted *complementary* color, assembled on a rotating disc, are in balance, if they blend into neutral gray. In the floral design the colors remain on their side of the central axis and continue to exert separate forces; on the rotating disc they move so fast that neither force registers separately on the eye, but only their combined force does, and this combined force is gray. Nor does it contradict the simple guide learned under proportion, i.e., a small amount of strong color, more of moderate color, and most of weak color makes for good color proportion. Instead, this analysis bears out that proportion is concerned with amount of color, balance with placement. The amount of color used has no bearing on balance, only its placement has.

This is not to say that stimulating colors should always be used near the central axis, but that color should be recognized for the force it exerts in relation to other colors and be used accordingly.

IMPACT OF TEXTURE

Since texture modifies color value, texture has a bearing on visual weight and consequently on balance. Rough textures, since they create shadows, make all colors darker and heavier.

Shiny textures, since they increase light reflection, increase the stimulating force of all colors.

The shiny blue surface must be reassessed in relation to a dull textured red; a shiny gray (silver) against a rough yellow. In fact, the impact of texture may be so great as to completely reverse the stimulating or releasing effect of certain colors, and their effect on balance.

The in-between textures have little effect on color balance.

IMPACT OF LIGHT AND SHADOW

Light from directly above casts shadows immediately below with accumulated shadows on the supporting surface. These add weight low, and add stability.

When the source of light is from one side only, one side will be light, the other dark. The dark side will seem heavier not only because of the lower value but because the space adjoining is dark and adds its weight to the foreground forms.

Light from below casts shadows above. It decreases the weight of the lower forms, and increases those higher up.

Because light does not normally come from below, its psychological effect opens a field for experimentation.

Since mankind is subject to the force of gravity and to actual balance, he is conditioned to respond to visual balance. However, as in the case of other principles, particularly contrast, we accept balance without being consciously aware of it. It is only when unbalance is a disturbing factor that we become aware of it and react thereto.

Rhythm

Rhythm is the organization of directional forces, of and between design elements, to induce dominant and subordinate eye movement within the design.

There is, of course, no actual movement of elements in design, except in mobiles—only eye movement stimulated by design elements and relationships between elements.

Direction is movement into space. Rhythm is a dominant direction established by inherent direction, by repetition, or by repetition with variation, and subordinate direction established by variation and/or contrast.

Why do we need or want rhythm in an arrangement?

Objects at rest are peaceful or static. Objects in motion are forceful and dynamic. The design lacking rhythm is static; the design that has rhythm, as on page 143 is dynamic! Since elements in design do not actually move about, we establish *visual movement*.

How can we control the design elements to create the feeling of rhythm? One direction should be dominant. It may be direction of line, form, color, or a combination thereof. Dominant direction of line and form are clearly established in the design on page 142. Other subordinate directions should support the dominant one.

CONTROLLING DIRECTION TO CREATE RHYTHM

Direction can be controlled to create dominant and subordinate rhythm by:

1. Selection of components, having the required inherent direction.

2. Altering direction of components. (Both of these are covered in the chapter on Direction.)

3. Modifying direction while placing it in design.

4. Relating to other directions already established.

MODIFYING DIRECTION

Directional forces present in plant material will carry over into the ultimate design, as in the design on page 118. This direction is modified as we hold it, place it on the holder, or secure it in any other part of the design. Coming from the point of support the material must be extended in some direction. It must go upward, downward, forward, backward, sideways, diagonal, or somewhere.

When the wisteria vine, the arrowhead leaf, or the rose is cut, then held in the hand, or impaled on the needlepoint holder, its direction from the point of support modifies the direction of every other point or area of this piece of plant material. The horizontal curve with an upward extending tip, typical of many lower branches of shrubs and trees, remains a curve, but becomes a downward pointing tip when placed upright on a holder.

The straight vertical direction of the cattail becomes a straight diagonal when placed at an angle on the holder. The right hand curve of the eucalyptus spray remains a curve, but becomes a left hand curve when placed to extend downward.

The inherent direction of any material carries over into the ultimate design, but is modified by the arranger as she places it.

Dominant rhythm. The directional force inherent in components carries over into the design. The diminishing form of the container and the circular line create dominant rhythmic movement, with all other directional lines subordinate to it.

Proportion. Bringing plant material across portions of the container reduces the visual size of the container and thereby changes its proportion to the plant material.

Harmony. The form of the container suggests the placement of the plant material and the form of the design.

Rhythm. Each element contributes to the dominant directional movement through the design, with contrasting but lesser movement to sustain interest.

RELATING DIRECTION

The most important line, which usually establishes the dominant direction, is generally placed first because all other lines are related to it.

Which is the most important line in an arrangement? It is always the one that has the greatest attraction. It is the largest, longest, most interesting variation of direction, etc. In the design on page 103, the wisteria vine starting at upper left and descending to lower right is the longest line. Its strength is augmented by the placement of the three poppies and the downward movement of the wisteria blossoms. This long and strong line becomes the "primary" line. Much consideration should be given to the primary line to which all others are to be related.

As this first line is placed on the holder, the arranger determines the direction in which it is to extend in *relation to the container*. Each additional placement must be considered in relation to the first placement, to the container, and each placement already made. Other placements should be related to the dominant one, but should have lesser force. Other strong lines, no matter how interesting in themselves, will tend to counteract and neutralize. If you have been guided by the principle of proportion in establishing the lengths of lines, you will have one rhythmic force that is stronger than the rest, and others that have lesser rhythm.

The flower arranger often starts with a branch, as on page 149, vine, or a piece of driftwood that has interesting variation of direction and allows it to suggest—even dictate—other placements.

Keeping lines close together as they emerge from the container results in a strong directional movement, often the strongest in the whole design. If the direction is vertical, the result is an upward thrust. The arrangement in a compote or narrow vertical container gains momentum from the upward directional strength of the stem or of the entire container. This force is continued up and augments the force of lines of plant material. If the lines above the container radiate, the force supplied by the container is soon dissipated.

Keeping curved lines together and extending in the same direction as they emerge from the container results in stronger movement as may be seen in the designs on pages 32 and 33. They may then change to variation of direction as they reach out through the design.

In order that rhythmic forces in design be dominant, these forces must be stronger than the static forces of a number of bold forms. Often the placement of contained forms weakens the established rhythm. We must then strengthen the linear forces, weaken the static forces, or reorganize material so that any contained forms become a part of the strong directional movement, rather than a competing one. In the design on page 109 the bold forms of the hibiscus are a part of the strong directional movement. When the dominant line is strengthened, supporting lines may appear weaker proportionately, so in turn will need reinforcing.

STRUCTURAL RHYTHM SUPPORTED BY CHROMATIC RHYTHM

Because our visual response to color is more direct and immediate than our response to form, it becomes important that color rhythm supports the structural design. Thus the dominant directional movement of all elements should be co-ordinated so that they support each other, rather than exert opposite forces. In the design on page 174 the dominant color of pale pink of both the apple blossoms and magnolia buds and blossoms support the dominant directional movement of the branch.

DOMINANCE TO PREVENT CONFUSION

Strong directional movement of too many different elements results in confusion. Two bold sansevieria leaves extending to the right, six iris in a vertical line, and six carnations, in gradations from pink to red, on the left, distracts in several directions, and is confusing. Since rhythm is a dominant movement with subordinate movement, too many strong directional movements is equivalent to no rhythm.

VARIATION AND CONTRAST TO PREVENT MONOTONY

Too much of the same kind of movement results in monotony. Again the result is no rhythm because it lacks subordinate movement.

Too many directions of similar lines, or several series of repetition of form, or similar color gradations of several hues, become tiresome. No matter how soothing or interesting a musical number may be, if the record sticks, and the same rhythm is repeated over and over, our response is "Turn that thing off!"

Rhythm is the organization of forces to create visual movement which contributes to dynamic floral design.

Dynamic Balance

CO-ORDINATION OF BALANCE AND RHYTHM

Balance is a state of rest. It is the co-ordination of the downward pull of gravity on all elements in design. It may involve *one* downward pull of gravity as in a horizontal arrangement of fruit, or in the heavy downward pull of a broad container. It may involve the opposition of *two* downward forces counterbalanced about a central axis.

Rhythm is motion. It is dominant movement. It may be in any direction—vertical, horizontal, diagonal, backward, forward or downward.

The distinctive arrangement is the one that co-ordinates these two opposing forces successfully.

Since rhythm is the active force—the one that expresses vitality—and balance the static force, we use rhythm to fully express a forceful design, with balance only as a counterpoise to stabilize it.

The co-ordination of balance and rhythm may be compared to actual co-ordination of balance and motion:

Symmetrical balance is similar to standing still—feet firmly planted and reverse weights equally distributed.

Asymmetrical balance, to walking—a balance of shifting weight, weight always supported alternately on one foot then the other.

Rhythm, by repetition, to dancing—a rhythmic movement from one area to another, but weight still supported alternately.

Rhythm, by diagonal line direction, to running—fast motion, both feet off the ground at the same time.

Dynamic balance, to skating or cycling—a co-ordination of balance and rhythm of diagonal line direction.

DYNAMIC BALANCE

Dynamic balance is the equilibrium of the opposing visual forces of balance and rhythm.

Dynamic balance should not be confused with asymmetrical balance. Asymmetrical balance deals with one force—the force of gravity as manifested in visual weight. Dynamic balance is the equilibrium of *two different forces*.

BALANCE OF TWO RHYTHMS

Two rhythmic lines of equal length, one moving down on one side and the other moving up on the other side do not balance each other. The force of gravity augments the downward direction. At the same time it reduces the force of the upward direction. Thus the downward line seems heavier.

Unequal directional lines on either side can balance each other. Shorter rhythmic lines moving down on one side from the point of support will balance longer ones moving up on the other side, as may be seen in the arrangement on page 149. The force of gravity reduces the upward force, but is added to the downward one. In analyzing designs incorporating the Hogarth curve, you will find that in the best examples the upper curve is usually the longer one.

Dynamic Balance. The angle of the branch and the bounding deer suggest dynamic motion strong enough to overcome the force of gravity. Thus the visual weight on the left need not be counterbalanced by similar visual weight on the right.

DIRECTION vs. WEIGHT

Directional force on one side of a central axis can be balanced by visual weight on the other side. The directional force may be upward and away from the point of support; the force of weight counteracts with a downward pull.

The common use of grapes, cascading down over the side of a stemmed or tall container, furnishes a diminishing line which provides both a downward weight and a downward movement to counterbalance strong upward movement on the other side.

The horizontal fruit and vegetable arrangement which is often a static heap on a wide base and which does not trigger a response in the viewer, can be imbued with tension and vitality through rhythm of form and color in the fruit or vegetables themselves and the use of linear material and foliage to continue this movement. The introduction of linear forms, which also means a change in dimension, results in better proportion. What was a hopeless pile, fit only for the home refrigerator, can be turned into a distinctive design by the establishment of a rhythmic force that lifts and vitalizes the whole design.

BALANCE BY WEIGHT OF CONTAINER

There may be strong directional movement with planned unbalance in the plant material as a unit, and this creates a strong tension; nevertheless this tension can be ultimately counterbalanced by heavy weight in the container.

We are attracted to a tree leaning out over a pond because of its tensional pull, but we know it will not fall because it is anchored deep in the earth. A floral design can produce the same effect: A leaning or cascading branch, seemingly out of balance, will create a similar tensional pull; yet the whole design can be in balance if the plant material is anchored in a heavy container which furnishes the necessary counterbalance. The heavy weight of the container may be real or only visual. Thus purposeful unbalance of strong linear material is introduced to create tension, but this unbalance is compensated for by great weight in the container.

Often the distinction of a design attributed to asymmetrical balance really stems from unbalance of visual weight. It is the tension created by a strong directional line that is not counter-balanced by plant material. To this the eye responds irresistably. It is, however, balanced by great weight in the container. If the same line were counterbalanced by plant material or supported at the other end, the stimulating force would be entirely lost.

THE FORCE OF RHYTHM

When the feeling of dynamic motion has been created, we can attain a sense of equilibrium without balance of visual weight. The following examples—from areas outside of floral design—will bear out this seeming contradiction.

The bicycle, although a perfectly balanced mechanism, will seldom stand alone. Put the bicycle into *motion,* then it may even lean without falling. A skater *in motion* can seemingly defy the law of gravity. In fact, not only can the rider or skater lean at an angle— he must lean at an angle when going around a curve so that gravity will exert a stronger force to counteract the force of tangent motion. What happens in each case is that the force of motion has overcome the force of gravity. The design on page 146 suggests the swift motion of a bounding deer. The force of dominant rhythm has overcome the force of gravity.

When we unleash the force of rhythm that equals or overcomes the force of gravity as in the design on page 180, then rhythm controls the design. This is often a key to distinction or expression in floral design.

Dynamic balance is achieved thru the co-ordination of the opposing forces of balance and rhythm.

Balance proves to be a principle of many facets. These range from static balance thru intermediate stages to dynamic balance; from the counterbalance of two individual elements through the tensions created by unequal elements of size, form, space, color, and/or texture, to those of strong opposing forces.

The arranger who controls the design elements, by means of the principles, to do her bidding, has become the master of her medium.

Co-ordination of Balance and Rhythm. The long upward line is balanced by the shorter downward line because the force of gravity reduces the upward force, but is added to the downward force.

Harmony. The interesting linear form of the primary line suggested other lines and the form of the ultimate design.

Related Color Harmony. Rhythm by repetition and variation of hue, value, and chroma.
Dominance of light values.

PART FIVE

OBJECTIVES, ET CETERA

OBJECTIVES OF DESIGN

STYLES OF FLOWER ARRANGING

JUDGING

GLOSSARY

Color Harmony Suggested by the Dominant Plant Material. The color harmony was suggested by the stimulating orange-red celosia. Contrast of lower value of green in coleus. Repetition of green of reduced chroma in background.

Related Color Harmony. Rhythm by repetition and variation of hue, value, and chroma.

Dominance of converging pattern in bold forms.

Complementary Harmony. The result of contrast of yellow-green and violet.

Decorative Design. The design elements of the plant material and container are co-ordinated with the design elements of the background. One enhances the other.

Objectives of Design

Let us re-examine our definition of flower arranging to ascertain its **objectives.**

Flower arranging is the art of organizing design elements, inherent in cut plant material and such other components as may be related thereto, **with intent to induce an aesthetic appeal.**

Design is but the means. Aesthetic appeal is the objective. Harmony, Distinction and Beauty are the attributes of aesthetic design.

Harmony is agreement among the component parts that results in an aesthetic whole. The ultimate design should have harmony in the relationship of its parts and interesting form of the whole design. Both are necessary and interdependent. Since each design consists of a structural design and a chromatic design, there should be harmony within each and between the two.

STRUCTURAL HARMONY

Heretofore we have been concerned with the form of the component parts. We are now concerned with the form of the whole design. As form is inherent in each part, so it is inherent in every grouping of parts. Every arrangement has form. It is never a question of form vs. no form, but rather what shall the form be.

The arranger can control the ultimate form by:

1. A predetermined plan.

2. An evolving plan.

THE PREDETERMINED FORM

The predetermined form is one that is completely planned in the mind of the arranger and constructed accordingly. Since the ultimate design is a form in space, the space the arrangement is to occupy may require a form similar to and in proportion to this space. In this case, however, the proportion of the space will be carried over into the design and the design will be in good or poor proportion accordingly.

While the ultimate form is established within a given space, the smaller spatial areas therein are being defined at the same time. The outlines of the physical components should establish both interesting form and interesting space.

A design need not be a geometric form or be spaced within its confines. It need not define or suggest the triangle, square, or circle; nor the pyramid, cube, or sphere; nor portions thereof. All these forms have *equal dimensions* previously discussed in the study of proportion. We know that a space as broad as it is tall and filled with plant material never won a blue ribbon at a flower show. The *less* the design looks like a triangle, square, circle, pyramid, cube, or sphere, the more interesting it will be.

When the definite form of the design is pre-planned, whether a geometric form or any other pre-planned form, the result is often stiff and stilted. Harmony, distinction and beauty are often sacrificed for conformance.

The form of every outstanding design, whether in art, fashion, or architecture, was first envisioned in the mind of the designer, each within the possibilities of its own medium. This is also true of floral design. However, it is highly probable that the image of the design originally in the mind of the arranger is changed, before final execution, more than that of any other art form. This is due to the fact that we are working with pre-organized material.

THE EVOLVING FORM

Let the material suggest the design. Let an interesting piece of plant material as on page 149 or the container as on pages 74, 142 or 159 suggest the design. An interesting piece is one in which form, color, and texture have already been organized into aesthetic relationship. Its form and color will suggest or even dictate what can be combined with it.

CHROMATIC HARMONY

A color plan is a predetermined combination of specific colors. Color harmony is the *result* of the application of design principles to the chromatic elements.

Since every design is a composite of a structural design and a chromatic design, *every* class in a flower show is a "color class."

Color harmony may be achieved by:

1. A predetermined plan.

2. An evolving plan.

When a class calls for a predetermined color plan, such as "an analogous arrangement," or "an arrangement with values of red predominating," the limitations imposed on the arranger are even greater than in the case of the predetermined form. The use of color masks on a color chart to blot out other colors on the chart are mechanical helps to selection of colors within specific limits. Let a class call for a specific color plan and it immediately sets up a block—a mental block in the mind of the arranger, and a physical block in regard to availability of material. Since color in plant material is so variable, and supply so unpredictable, the problem becomes a frustrating one. Available flowers

When the arranger is concerned with bringing the structural elements into harmonious relationship within the design, the ultimate form evolves. The form of the design evolves while the elements are being brought into harmony. You may not be able to identify it by a geometric term or other name, but this form will have a character all its own and there will be harmony of the whole.

UNITY

Unity is seldom a problem in flower arranging. The physical nature of plant material which requires a means of support such as the container, or the holder in the container, the controlling mechanics on a corsage etc., though mechanical in nature, help to achieve unity. The bringing together of the plant material and container at one point or to one common component, such as a base, gives cohesion to the design without conscious striving for unity on the part of the arranger. If unity is lacking, it is usually caused by the introduction of diverse elements of optional components.

seldom conform to a specific color plan. The arranger usually becomes so concerned about conformance, that she loses sight of all other considerations. Good form is often sacrificed in order to stay within the limitations of the color plan. The predetermined color plan, although the stock-in-trade of the interior decorator, makes flower arranging more difficult without making it better.

THE EVOLVING COLOR PLAN

In the evolving procedure the arranger starts with a color she wishes to emphasize. This may be in the container, background, or in some plant material as in the design on page 153. She then relates other colors to it as the design progresses. These relationships will usually be more pleasing than the forced combinations in the predetermined plan.

The normal psychological response to color as outlined in the chapter on Chromatic Elements is so strongly developed in the arranger who has good taste or "a feeling for design" that she selects color and uses it effectively without conscious effort. However, it is probably more correct to say that because she lets her psychological response guide her in selection and use of color, that she has good taste, and "a feeling for design."

The form of the design is suggested by the form of the container.

PRINCIPLES APPLIED TO CHROMATIC ELEMENTS

The chapter on Chromatic Elements analyzed the force that individual colors exert on the viewer. In design, however, we are concerned with combination of all colors of all components. Color, the same as other elements, can be combined in only three ways: repetition and/or variation and/or contrast. Proportion and direction are inherent in all combinations.

Color harmony results from the co-ordination of these inherent relationships.

Color dominance co-ordinates repetition, variation and proportion of hue or value, with variation or contrast of subordinate color.

Color balance co-ordinates repetition, variation, contrast, proportion and direction of color.

Color rhythm co-ordinates repetition, variation and direction of color.

RELATED HARMONIES

Rhythm of color is important to a related color harmony. Rhythm that consists of repetition of hue with repetition and variation of value and chroma, and no contrast of color results in a monochromatic harmony. Rhythm that consists of repetition and variation in value, chroma, *and* hue, and no contrast of color results in an analogous harmony. In related harmonies subordinate color is a variation of the dominant color, as seen in the designs on pages 150 and 154. With no contrast of color, greater contrast of other elements need to be provided in order to maintain interest. Contrast of structural elements and of texture must supply the necessary impact of contrast lacking in color, as in the design on page 86.

If we want the background to be part of the related color harmony, we can use any color in the design or a closely related one. However, a value that is either darker or lighter than any in the design gives better definition to structural elements. If the background should be gray then it is advisable to use a background of very weak chroma of the dominant hue, or add some of the dominant hue to neutral gray, rather than using neutral gray alone. In the chapter on Color Factors it was pointed out that any strong chroma becomes weaker after a few minutes of observation. The eye grays a hue by supplying the complementary hue. A strong red in front of a gray background induces the complementary green, so that the neutral gray gradually appears greenish, giving the effect of a contrasting color plan by placement, rather than a completely related plan.

Hues between the warm or cool portions of the color circle may assume changing aspects. When yellow-green is combined with green and blue-green it has the effect of a cool color; if combined with yellow and yellow-orange it becomes a warm color. If on the other hand yellow-green is combined with green, blue-green, blue, and blue-violet, the color interval between yellow-green and blue-violet is so great, that yellow-green will act as a warm contrast to blue-violet. If yellow-green is combined with yellow, yellow-orange, orange, and red-orange, it will be a cool contrast to red-orange.

HARMONY OF CONTRASTING HUES

Contrast of hue results in a complementary harmony. Complementary hues are opposite or nearly opposite each other on the color circle. Opposites vary with different color systems. What is a complement on one circle is a near-complement on another. The design on page 155 contrasts violet with yellow-green.

Incorporating a contrasting hue into a monochromatic harmony changes it into a complementary harmony. Incorporating a contrasting hue of any one color of an analogy into it, results in an analogous complementary. The analogous complementary is particularly adapted to the luxuriant montage in which the color splendor of flowers can be exploited to the fullest.

CONTRAST OF VALUE AND CHROMA

White and black, very light red and very dark red, yellow and black, green and white, are all examples of contrast of value. Technically very light red and very dark red are monochromatic. Any hue combined with white or black is also monochromatic because white and black are values of every hue, as on pps. 50, 51. In design, however, we are concerned with visual response and in each of the given examples the colors are one opposite ends of the value scale. The visual impact of contrast is much greater than the effect of likeness or near likeness.

There is stronger contrast between yellow and black than between yellow and white, because yellow, at its greatest intensity, is further removed from black than from white. Conversely, there is greater contrast between blue or purple and white than black because their greatest intensity is further from white.

It would appear that red and green being about equidistant from black and white should be in equal harmony with either; however, because red and white are both stimulating colors, green and black both releasing colors, dominance and resulting harmony is easier to establish with a contrast of red and black, or a contrast of green and white.

Full chroma, as usually found in flowers, against a grayed background furnishes a contrast of chroma. Most flowers against most foliage (being grayed-green) also furnishes a contrast of chroma.

The above "named" harmonies are but a portion of the many that can be created. Most subtle and interesting color harmonies are "name-less." The design that shouts its color relationship is often the one that lacks a strong structural design. Color should be so closely integrated with form in the ultimate design that the mind receives but one impression.

Structural harmony and chromatic harmony, both attributes of aesthetic design, are the result of consilience of design principles.

DISTINCTION

Distinction starts with good design, but it is also dependent on many other factors.

Webster defines distinction as "State or quality of being distinguishable or distinct." This not only allows us but compels us to ask and then supply the information, "from what?" and "in what respect?"

Distinct from what? From other components in the same general area. The answer to this certainly varies with the place in which the design is shown. Is it shown individually, as in the home? Or is it shown in the flower show where it is in competition with a multitude of other arrangements?

In what respect? Distinction is marked superiority in every respect. "In every respect" includes all factors, tangible and intangible, which may have a bearing on floral design, and which may apply at any given time. In the home, in the church, at the head table of a banquet hall, or other single placement area, the aspects that are relevant are different from and probably fewer than those to be considered in the flower show.

ASPECTS THAT MAY EFFECT DISTINCTION

1. Technical Perfection. This is truly the first requirement. The arranger must have exercised complete and skillful control over her medium in creating her design. An excellent choice of functional elements and an ingenious idea are but the raw materials in the hands of the arranger. Technical skill in the execution of the design will spell the difference between distinction, mediocrity, or tawdryness.

2. Condition. We are not always interested in condition in the same sense as the horticulturist; in fact, plant material in poor condition horticulturally may have great design possibilities. But condition factors that detract, such as wilt, soil, damage from weather or disease, would also detract from distinction.

3. Attracts attention. The design stimulates the eye and attracts attention to itself. If you must hunt for distinction, it isn't there. In the home the arrangement that is well related to and harmonious with its surroundings creates an area of accelerated interest, and readily achieves distinction. It need not compete with another arrangement, but need only be of greater interest than surrounding objects. If, for an example, a nearby picture distracts (another way of saying that it attracts attention to itself,) the arrangement will lack distinction.

In the flower show, however, it must complete successfully with many other arrangements. The arrangement that is in perfect balance and has the golden mean proportion may be harmonious and pleasing. You can observe it, enjoy it, but you can also leave it because it fails to hold you. The arrangement that has tension and attraction, that stimulates you, or may even haunt you, brings you back again and again to experience its compelling force.

4. Holds attention. The design must do more than stimulate to attract. It must be satisfying over a period of time. A bizarre or ugly arrangement may attract attention, but it will not be able to hold it.

5. Contrast. Repetition of the same material or manner of placement within an arrangement results in monotony. In the same manner, repetition of similar material, ideas or manner of execution of arrangements dulls the visual sense. Contrast rekindles interest. Such contrast is often achieved by refraining from the use of the obvious. Many a blue ribbon has gone to the arrangement of foliage in a class where all other entries contained flowers; and the tricolor to the foliage class where all other blue ribbon winners had flowers predominating. Conversely, in a cactus show the tri-color was awarded to an arrangement in the only class that contained flowers.

6. A new idea. Material and ideas that may be commonplace in one area may be unusual in another and create appeal. The looped wisteria vine that has been shown again and again may have distinction for the novice. Material that is commonplace in the tropics is considered exotic by those who have never been there. The container with three openings may appeal to the individual who is accustomed to the conventional one. The seedpods and stem pattern of the poisonous jimson weed, scorned by the rural members, may have distinction for the suburbanite. An idea or material, not new in itself, when introduced to those not familiar with it, has the same impact as an entirely new idea.

7. Creativity. This is the arranger's fresh approach to the choice of material or to the manner in which commonplace material is organized. Individuality is that intangible quality that sets one arrangement apart from the rest.

8. Satisfies aesthetically. The viewer should be able to return to the distinctive arrangement again and again and experience a renewed sense of pleasure each time. This, undoubtedly, is the main test: how rich and full is the experience for the viewer?

"Woodland Sprites." The design suggests that wide-eyed sprites emerge from hollow dead stumps.

EXPRESSION

Expression is a desirable attribute of design, but it is not an essential objective. If employed it is in *addition* to the basic attributes of pure design. Expression is that quality of design that communicates with the observer by conveying a mood, feeling, or theme. An emotion to be conveyed or a title to be interpreted broadens the scope of floral design. The design above interprets its title. Expression may serve as a challenge to the imaginative arranger. However, we must guard against the design that is merely expressive—that merely tells a story—but lacks the other attributes of good design. With these the question arises as to how much harmony, distinction, or beauty may be sacrificed to expression. We may acquiesce in lack of beauty, but we should never sanction ugliness. Ugliness repels. There is enough ugli-

ness in the world around us so there can be no excuse for creating more, under the guise of art.

BEAUTY

Beauty is that intangible quality that evokes aesthetic pleasure and delight.

Why should an arrangement be beautiful? Beauty gratifies an emotional need. An appreciation of beauty and the desire to create it, are our responses to this need.

There are those who believe that beauty for beauty's sake is a worthless endeavor. It is true that surface decoration to conceal ugliness or repulsiveness may be disdained; but anything that is beautiful in itself needs no excuse. Beauty has intrinsic worth.

Styles of Flower Arranging

Style is the characteristic manner of arranging. Principles remain unchanged, but styles in arranging, like styles in clothing, change periodically. Styles of arranging have risen like the crest of a wave, only to recede and give way to another.

Flower arranging styles can be classified from many perspectives, most of which overlap, and from each perspective there is no hard and fast line of demarcation between styles. We must consider the viewing point and realize that most arrangements may fall into more than one category, and within a category, their position as to style is relative.

The following are some of the perspectives from which flower arranging may be considered (there are others) and from which styles may be classified:

As to country of origin: European, Japanese, American.

As to time: period, traditional, modern, contemporary.

As to form: naturalistic, geometric, free form.

As to purpose: aesthetic, decorative, expressive, interpretive.

As to precept: the commercial florist;

Japanese schools of flower arranging;

the fine arts;

American Flower Show Schools.

There are very few characteristics that are peculiar to only one style. There is no style that stands out alone —each style shares some characteristics with some other style. So in designating various styles we are as much concerned with similarities as with distinct differences.

COUNTRY OF ORIGIN

In Europe and other countries under European influence, flower arranging has been sponsored through horticulture societies. In their exhibitions, horticulture with perfection of specimen is of prime importance, with arranging of subordinate interest.

Although a relatively new art form in the United States, flower arranging shares honors with horticulture in the activities of garden clubs. Flower arranging has become more popular in shows in the United States than in Europe, but in each flower arranging has developed along similar lines. Both are on an amateur basis and arrangements are in competition in the flower show.

In Japan flower arranging has existed for many centuries. Flower arranging exhibitions do not include horticulture. There is no competition between exhibits. There are no garden clubs in Japan. There are hundreds of schools—each with its own rules of arranging—and teaching is strictly on a professional basis. Since World War II Japanese styles of arranging together with other aspects of Japanese culture have been carried to all countries where there is an interest in horticulture, gardening or flower arranging.

In European exhibits emphasis is on mass arrangements; in Japan emphasis is on line arrangements. Both of these styles have been merged into the massed line design popular in the United States.

PERIOD ARRANGEMENTS

During the 17th, 18th, and early 19th century artists painted flower pictures. They showed bouquets of flowers in vases. The bouquet is a bunch of flowers grouped to show individual blooms to best advantage, with little regard to their relation to each other. A study of these paintings and contemporary prints shows that they do not portray real bouquets, much less real flower arrangements. We have little evidence that flower arranging, as we know it, existed in earlier centuries. "Period Arrangements" can only be adaptations of flower paintings, or arrangements showing the influence of a given historical period.

The so-called "Colonial Arrangement of wild flowers in a beanpot," is a modern concept. It is what *we* do with wild flowers and a beanpot. The colonial dame would not think of using "wild" flowers. We need go back only two or three generations to learn that wild flowers were considered weeds. The beanpot served a utilitarian purpose on the kitchen hearth—often the kitchen itself was not even a part of the house! Put flowers in the lowly cook pot? Never!

"Period arrangements" in earlier centuries consisted of mixed bouquets of garden flowers or greenhouse flowers, the latter from private greenhouses of the wealthy. In the 20th century flowers became available to the middle classes, from the commercial florist, so that the "florists dozen" became the usual medium. The dozen, or two or three dozen, were always the same variety at the same stage of development, which meant that ensuing design had but one size, form, color, texture, and pattern of flowers, with some "greens." Available holders or "frogs" predetermined the position of every stem, so that the pincushion design of one kind of flower become the accepted arrangement of the early twentieth century period. It still is a prevalent style outside of garden club or art circles.

TRADITIONAL vs. MODERN

There seems to be much divergence of opinion as to what is traditional or modern, and rightly so. Webster defines traditional as: "something handed down from the *past;* an inherited culture, attitude, etc." But what is "past" depends on the individual. Those who took part in developing a style that is still of current interest consider that style modern. A younger generation or a newer garden club member who arrives on the scene after a style has become established, considers the same style as having been handed down from the past. They, in turn, consider only the styles developed during their time of interest as modern. To some, everything except period is modern; to others, everything except abstract is traditional. On the other hand abstract art itself is traditional for it predates conventional flower arranging by several decades; but abstract flower arranging is modern.

When the term "modern" was first applied to flower arranging several decades ago it reflected the contemporary trends in furniture and interior decorating. These were characterized by use of bold size, line, form, color and/or texture, and by clean-cut geometric pattern. These characteristics distinguished the modern style of flower arranging from the conventional flower arranging with which it was contemporary. Conventional flower arranging used any kind of plant material in a line, massed-line, or mass design.

When used alone, "modern" may still connote bold and uncluttered design; however, as newer styles develop they too apply the term "modern" such as "modern free form," "modern abstract," etc.

CONTEMPORARY

"Contemporary" is not a single style, but refers to a group of styles existing at the same time. When the term "contemporary" refers to a single style it implies a style of the present time. The following are all contemporary in that they are all "of the same time," and "of the present time": line, massed line, mass, modern, free form, free-style, expressive, abstract, and creative.

If an arrangement must be classified as to style, other categories, than traditional, modern, or contemporary are more meaningful.

NATURALISTIC STYLE

In the naturalistic style the arranger suggests the natural growth habit of the particular plant material used. An example would be one or more stalks of iris, with the largest flower up high, emerging from a fan of iris leaves.

GEOMETRIC STYLE

Geometric style is manifested in form or pattern. Designs that closely resemble a geometric figure, such as the triangle, square, circle, the pyramid, cube, or sphere are geometric in form. Linear portions of geometric figures are also geometric in form. Examples are the crescent, parabolic, right angled or vertical line.

The second aspect of geometric style is found in patterns within the form. Patterns of straight lines, bold forms, truncated forms, sharp angles, or sharp delineation of shapes and forms, are characteristic. Since strong or contrasting color accentuates form or pattern, their use creates a greater impact of geometric form or pattern than the use of weak or related colors might produce. The design on page 90 has geometric form.

Free Form Style. The design is suggested by the flowing lines of the bird figurine. Note that the greatest interest area is away from its conventional place above the point where the linear material emerges from the container.

It should be noted that the so-called "triangle" or "triangular arrangement," is seldom a triangle, nor does it have three angles. What is usually meant is a tri-linear arrangement, having three lines, four angles or spaces, and five sides. It may be naturalistic, geometric, or free form.

FREE FORM

Free-form design is neither naturalistic or geometric. It is outside of any traditional or conventional style or pattern. However, it may embody characteristics of one or more styles. In the design on page 63 natural and geometric forms are combined. On page 165 the greatest interest area is separated from the linear pattern. The design on the facing page does not conform to any conventional style.

The spaces established within free-form design are also free from restrictions. The only guidelines the exhibitor must observe—as always—are the principles of design. Since free-form allows the exhibitor greater freedom it also leads to more creative expression.

AESTHETIC DESIGN

Aesthetic design has but one purpose—to induce an aesthetic appeal in the observer. Flowers themselves are usually the inspiration for aesthetic design.

The gardener laboriously tends her garden throughout the seasons. When the time arrives that it abounds with flowers, comes the desire to enjoy them to the fullest. She has the desire to create beauty with the harvest from her garden. She arranges her flowers with no other motive except her own greater enjoyment and that of her family and friends.

The American home prides itself on its many built-in features. But it has no built-in area to display flower arrangements. There is no place in the American scheme of architecture wherein a flower arrangement can be "staged"—a place where space, color, lighting, or orientation are such that design is enhanced to the fullest of its aesthetic possibilities—a place where it can be appreciated as a work of art. The flower show attempts to furnish such staging, but being temporary and improvised, it often leaves much to be desired. Thus the flower arrangement in the home often becomes a decorative design.

DECORATIVE DESIGN

Decorative design is intended to enhance a given place or area. It is co-ordinated with its frame of reference and may be subordinate to other components. Examples are: an arrangement to complement a picture, a dinner or buffet table arrangement, a corsage, or an arrangement suitable for an entrance hall table. The design is but a part, either greater or lesser, of a larger whole. Its structural and chromatic design are suggested by the form and color of the area to be embellished. The decorative design on page 156 is co-ordinated with its background, and each is enhanced by the other.

Both aesthetic and decorative styles have always been abstract to some extent. Both serve to create visual stimuli which induce psychological response. Neither attempts to represent something else, as in traditional painting or sculpture.

In co-ordinating the form and color of plant material with the form and color of the background, consideration of space has always been important, although formerly its importance was not always fully recognized. However, there is still greater emphasis on fluid space and partially enclosed space than on enclosed space.

EXPRESSIVE AND INTERPRETIVE DESIGN

The expressive design conveys the exhibitor's idea or mood. The interpretive design conveys a given idea, mood, theme, occasion, or atmosphere. Both are achieved through interpretation into the medium of plant material, as in the arrangement on the right.

The emotional response of the arranger to the components, and to their design elements, in addition to the visual response determines the selection and organization of the components. Since emotional response is largely dependent on the sum total of the individual's past experience, this response varies with the individual. In our study of emotional reaction to color we observed that a single color may evoke opposite emotions in different people. Thus the emotional response of the viewer may be the one intended to be conveyed by the arranger; again, it may be different or opposite; then again, the emotional response may be completely lacking.

Since a flower show should be educational, beautiful, and inspirational, the expressive design that carries no intent to communicate with the viewer has no place in the flower show. The value of any art, hobby, or

"Into Orbit." The ascending thrust suggested by the celosia carries the eye up into the orbit suggested by the spiraling wisteria stem.

other activity, to the individual as a means of self-expression cannot be denied or challenged, but if its purpose is merely self-expression, it should remain where it best serves its purpose—in the confines of the creator's inner sanctum.

The expressive design and the interpretive design, although not forms of "realism" art, do have many characteristics of representational art.

THE COMMERCIAL FLORIST

The florists designs, being commercial, are seldom included in a listing of flower arranging styles, yet they have made an indelible imprint on American culture. *The florist has created an American symbolism of flowers.* He has associated certain flowers and certain designs literally with occasions from the cradle to the grave. Tiny rosebuds belong to baby showers, large "mums" to football games, orchids to formal parties, and orange blossoms to weddings. The pincushion design of pink roses in crystal or silver is a symbol of the formal dinner table; the fan-shaped design of gladiolus, a symbol of the funeral parlor. "Easter" lilies belong to Easter; poinsettias, holly and other evergreens to Christmas.

In one respect this has created more widespread enjoyment of flowers in the home and elsewhere. But in another respect, it has been unfortunate that flowers have thus been typed and their use limited. Such associations once established are difficult to divorce. It is with this background of symbolism that the average gardener becomes interested in flower arranging. As one novice arranger once inquired, "May I use pine or holly in April?" Slowly, however, the arranger arrives at a different perspective. She may still use flowers symbolically should the occasion demand, but she can also divest them of the past company they have been keeping and see them as units in design.

JAPANESE SCHOOLS OF FLOWER ARRANGING

Some of the outstanding characteristics of the classical Japanese style are use of odd numbers, symbolism, asymmetry, dominance of line, and rules based on the principles of proportion and direction.

Each Japanese school has its own set of rules. However, it is significant to note that all Japanese rules are based on the two inherent principles of proportion and direction. Proportion is expressed as a numerical ratio: the first piece of plant material in relation to the container; other pieces in relation to the first placement. Direction in plant material is modified; examples: bending of lines, highest tip directly over the base, etc. Relative direction of two or more placements is specifically controlled to establish asymmetry and depth; examples: "in front of," "at a 30 degree angle," "toward the right shoulder," etc.

These specific rules coupled with instruction in technique are a boon to the beginner who is at a complete loss as to where or how to start. These rules may later serve as general guides.

Emphasis on the element of line has resulted in appreciation of good linear structure. Form, color, and texture are of secondary importance. They must always be subordinated so that the linear elements remain dominant. It would probably be more correct to say that form, color and texture are considered only because they are inherent in the plant material. Chromatic elements are seldom organized so as to achieve color harmonies.

All Japanese styles are asymmetric in form. This does not mean that all designs have asymmetric balance. More often than not, the greatest visual impact is exerted by the tension created by planned unbalance.

Symbolism, closely associated with Japanese history, culture and social structure, is meaningful in Japan. By its very nature, it bears no relation to American cultural and social values, or to American flower arranging.

The Japanese tokonoma is an architectural feature built for the express purpose of supplying a "stage" for floral designs. Unfortunately, an American counterpart does not exist. The idea could well be considered by American homemakers and architects.

THE FINE ARTS

In the realm of painting and sculpture, we find that art can be classified into two broad categories: representational art and abstract art. Both styles use mediums that are *form-less.* The artist uses paint, clay, stone, plastic, cloth, etc., with which he creates form.

REPRESENTATIONAL ART

Representational art portrays visual likeness. The painter depicts three-dimensional forms of subjects or scenes on a two-dimensional surface. The sculptor molds a physical form similar in contour to a natural one. Among other subjects, they also portray flowers and other plant material.

ABSTRACT ART

The term "abstract" as defined in Webster's has several distinct meanings, some of which are opposite or contradictory. The following are several of these distinct meanings which have been applied to art and which indicate that *abstract art is not a single style, but consists of several styles:*

> " . . . considered apart from any application to a particular object or specific instance; having no reference to a thing or things."

The artist employing this concept creates *non-representational abstract* for he does not portray recognizable subject matter. He creates and uses form and color solely as units in design and for its psychological impact. This abstract style expresses no ulterior meaning and makes no claim to beauty being its objective. The "crazy" patch quilt of grandmother's day was a *craft* that employed the same concept: forms, colors, and geometric patterns were organized for a striking effect.

> " . . . expressing a property, quality, attribute, or relation viewed apart from other characteristics inhering in or constituting an object." " . . . something that comprises or concentrates in itself the essential qualities of a larger thing or several things."

The Stabile of "Devil's Claws" impaled on contorted hydrangea stems emphasizes closed and partially enclosed space, and reflects the influence of abstract sculpture which employs the products of modern technology such as distorted metal shapes, plastic covered wire, etc.

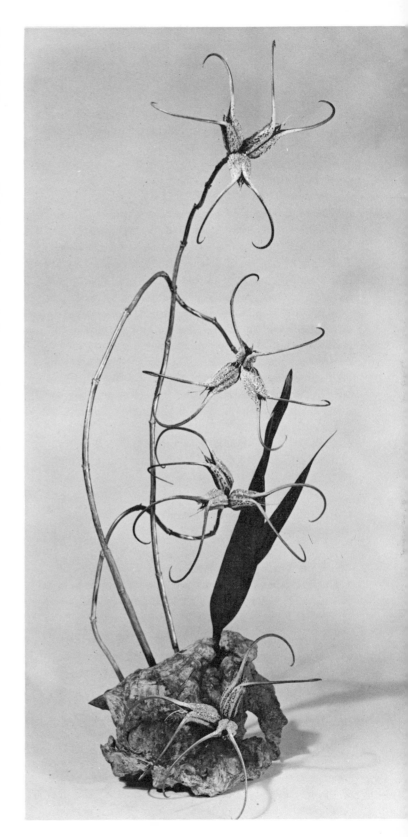

From these concepts has developed another style in which the artist depicts only important characteristics while eliminating the unimportant in design. Two flowing lines may represent a fish, with the unimportant scales, fins, etc., eliminated. This is *simplified characterization*.

" . . . presenting or possessing schematic or generalized form frequently suggested by and having obscure resemblance to natural appearance thru contrived ordering of pictorial or sculptural elements."

From this concept has developed a *subjective style* in which form or color is not used for itself, but for the associations it can bring up in the mind of the viewer. The form of a piece of scrap iron may resemble a starfish; that of a piece of driftwood may conjure up the outline of a bird or the head of a dog; a twisted stem may indicate a storm or inner turmoil. Components in design need not be related visually or functionally but are used as a means of interpreting an idea, theme, mood, emotion, or occasion. The design has a story to tell. The expression is not by means of a literal picture but thru interpretation of forms or colors which stimulate an emotional response in the viewer because he can associate them with his own experience. "Into orbit," on page 167 stimulates such a response. The communication with the viewer is more indirect and unobstrusive than in representational art.

All subjective abstract is expressive, but not all expressive design is abstract.

Note that one style breaks away from representation completely while the purpose of another is to create "an obscure resemblance to natural appearance."

Thus abstract art embodies several distinct styles, namely non-representational, simplified characterization, and subjective. Among them there is greater divergence than similarity.

INTEREST AREAS

In representational art there is normal perspective. Lines and extensions thereof meet and the eye is led to the meeting point or focal area. In non-representational abstract the artist is not concerned with perspective and consequently *there is no single focal area.* Instead, interest is focused on the whole design.

On the other hand, when the artist eliminates details in simplified characterization and "concentrates on essential qualities," he also *concentrates interest within certain areas.* Likewise, the artist who communicates an idea, theme, etc., is more likely to concentrate interest than to distribute it throughout the design.

In focusing interest on the whole design or while creating several tension areas throughout the design, the arranger should never lose sight of the fact that the principle of dominance applies to abstract design as well as to conventional design. Too often the arranger's effort to create interest throughout the design results in disorder and confusion.

ABSTRACT MEDIUM vs.
ABSTRACT STYLE

Plant material, since it is preorganized, does not lend itself to true representational style. On the other hand, flower arranging, as we have practiced it within the last several decades, has been essentially abstract, in that *we have used plant material solely for its form and color.* We did not however arrange in the styles of the abstract artists who use paint, clay and other mediums. We arranged in the conventional line, massed line, and massed styles.

Recently, however, the styles of the abstract artists have been adapted to plant material. The stabile on page 169 shows the influence of abstract sculpture. The medium of plant material does lend itself, in some degree, to both the subjective abstract style where its "obscure resemblance" is used to interpret subjective feeling into form and color, and to the non-representational abstract style where interest is focused on the whole design.

ASSEMBLAGE

An assemblage is a grouping of diverse units. Each unit although generally complete in itself, becomes a component of a larger and more complex design. The units may be related visually thru inherent design elements, and/or emotionally thru association of ideas.

Thus an assemblage, like any other floral design, may reflect various styles. It may be aesthetic, decorative, expressive or interpretative; it may be traditional, modern, or abstract, etc. The assemblage on page 63 relates its units thru repetition of form, color, and texture, and to a lesser extent, thru association of ideas.

Creative Design. Strong focal area is combined with abstract forms, geometric lines, and spaces. Mechanics are integrated into design. Strong contrast of line emphasizes spaces created by it.

MONTAGE

The montage is a modern art form which starts with visual excerpts, each of which conveys a brief message, which are combined in such a manner that the eye follows one message after another, so that the mind receives them as a co-ordinated whole.

This is sometimes done with portions of pictures—just that part that gets across the desired message — mounted on a background in a circle, or other combination that is easily followed. Sometimes it is done on a screen, in much the same manner, with overlapping images. Often it is applied in a time sequence—rather than a space sequence—with consecutive flashes of scenes. The latter is the form frequently used on television commercials.

Applying this concept to flower arranging we start with the medium of plant material, of which each unit is already organized according to design principles—and which already has aesthetic appeal—then organize these pre-organized units into the ultimate design, as on page 175, for even greater interest and distinction. The massed design on page 173 employs the same concept.

The montage makes the most of the *difference* between flower arranging and the other visual arts. Both painting and sculpture start with formless mediums—paint and clay are unorganized and in themselves lack beauty and distinction.

There does exist a modern form of sculpture or assemblage, in which pre-organized forms, such as pieces of old cars or baby buggies, and other items from the junk yard, are organized into an art form of sorts. However, these things lack aesthetic appeal—and most often the finished product does also!!

Although the floral montage is put together similar to the montage in other art forms, it is also a truly abstract design. Form and color are organized purely for their visual and psychological impact. There is no effort to tell a story—to arouse an emotion—or to represent or portray anything else. It also has interest distributed throughout the design—a characteristic which it shares not only with abstract design, but with the period bouquet.

Flowers, branches, vines, and other plant material are particularly adapted to the montage style, *for each retains its identity and beauty while contributing its form and color to the ultimate design*. The montage allows the arranger to exploit the sensuous beauty of individual flowers, while blending their elements into a harmonious whole.

We are indebted to the representational artist for our appreciation of design. We have learned about color from the painter, about form from the sculptor. We are indebted to the abstract artist for our apprecittion of creativeness. The design on page 169 shows the influence of abstract art on flower arranging. We have recognized design elements and principles as the ·means through which the artist communicates with the viewer. We have learned from these older arts, and we take what can be applied to our medium of plant material and the art of floral design.

AMERICAN FLOWER SHOW SCHOOLS

American Flower Show Schools place emphasis on design elements as manifested in plant material and on design principles as they are applied to the same. The beginner starts with specific design plans and color plans which can be readily grasped, and by means of which design principles are exemplified. The line, massed line, and the massed design, as illustrated on pages 174, 180 and 173 respectively, are useful in establishing a concept of design principles as they apply to structural design. The related color plans, as on pages 20, 86, 150 and 154, and the contrasting color plans, as on pages 103 and 155 are likewise useful to an understanding of design principles as they apply to chromatic design.

After the arranger has learned to control plant material, has learned to recognize the visual forces exerted by design elements, and how to control these forces by means of design principles, she can create floral design freely, within or outside of established styles.

Massed Design, with some line interest; typical of American style. Also has characteristics of the modern montage.

Chromatic Rhythm Supports Structural Rhythm. The dominant color of pale pink of both the apple blossoms and magnolia buds and blossoms support the dominant directional movement of the branch.

Montage. The Montage combines preorganized form and color of components into a harmonious whole for greater interest and distinction, while each unit retains its design entity.

"FREE-STYLE"

Unfortunately the term "free-style", an American term applied by the Japanese to their current style of arranging, has often been applied to floral designs which have broken away from the conventional, the fixed style, or the stereotyped arrangement.

However, the term itself is a contradiction. To be a style it must have acquired certain distinguishing characteristics, which then identify it, so cannot be free. If it is a completely free form of expression, it cannot be a style.

CREATIVE FLORAL DESIGN

The term "Creative Floral Design," expresses the goal of most arrangers. It affirms the idea that design is basic—that it is the foundation on which this art form rests. It indicates that *flora*—as distinguished from *fauna* or inorganic material—is the medium which is used, or through which the arranger expresses herself. It conveys the thought that design results from an inspiration within the mind of the arranger. It implies freedom in selection of material and freedom in the manner in which it is organized.

Creative floral design may embody some characteristics of one or more established styles, but is unhampered by adherence to any one style, predetermined form, or color plan.

It may begin with the elements or principles in the dominant plant material, such as its line or its proportion, and let these suggest or control the design as on pages 135 and 167. It can begin with the most stimulating color and let it determine what can be used with it. It may range from the severely restrained style in which pure line structure furnishes the dominant interest, to the luxuriant montage. It may remain within or outside of any style or it may combine characteristics of one style with those of another as in the design on page 171. In short, *the arranger is free to create design* within the limitations of her medium and those of her artistic ability.

It should be noted, however, that any established style or creative design is *not* synonymous with *good* design. We will find good, fair, and poor design in each of them.

CREATIVITY

Not all arrangers are endowed with the same degree of inspiration or creativeness. Nor can we suddenly decide to become creative. However, conscious effort can be made to stimulate creative thinking and expression.

If you have developed your own style as a result of repeatedly adhering to instructions, rules, codes, and "What they say," you may find it difficult to break away—just as it is difficult to break away from any other fixed habit.

Freedom of expression can be consciously cultivated by making one distinct break after another. Try combining plant material you have never used together before. Try new color combinations. Place material in or on the container or on the base in a different manner as on page 142 or on page 165. Note that in the latter design the focal area has been moved away from its conventional place. The several openings in the container on the right stimulated a new approach. Use a receptacle or other thing you have never thought of using as a container. Combine containers or bases as on page 63. Combine geometric form with free form, etc.

It may take real mental effort, and the result may not be good at first. But gradually the dependency on what you have done in the past—the old tried and true flowers, containers, and styles—becomes less. Mental inhibitions become less, so that you can exercise greater freedom in choice of components, in combination of elements, and in the manner in which they are related. You will have taken an important step toward expressing yourself freely, which is a prerequisite to creativity.

Such a preconceived conscious plan to gain freedom of expression should not be confused with the beginner's effort who does not know what she is striving to accomplish, nor how to go about it. The beginner who combines material at random has nothing to guide her, while the arranger who has studied the design principles, and has assimilated them, finds that they guide her subconsciously.

Creative Design. A container with openings at several levels poses a challenge to the arranger. (Container by Mrs. C. W. Thomas.)

Judging

Being an arranger does not automatically make for being a good judge. The arranger develops into a judge thru a dual process:

1. By detaching herself from her own work so she can view it impersonally.

2. By developing the faculty of experiencing fully the work of others.

When we create a floral design, we are so emotionally involved in our own creation—our brain child—that it is difficult to see its merits or demerits objectively. When our work is poor, we do not know it and our best friend won't tell us. Only painful self analysis will help. A helpful procedure is to photograph the arrangement in color, black and white, or both. Six months later the emotional involvement has disintegrated and the arrangement can be viewed dispassionately and objectively. The design on which we once pinned tricolor hopes now appears in its true version—some good points but also some glaring faults. By this method we can pass unbiased judgment on our own work. This is an important step toward improving our design and an even more important step toward becoming a good judge. It tends to deflate the ego and develop an open mind—basic requirements for a good judge.

THE JUDICIAL TEMPERAMENT DEVELOPS

The beginning arranger who is also aspiring to become a judge passes through the following phases while attempting to judge the work of others. The advanced arranger who becomes interested in judging starts somewhere along the series.

Phase One: Sees only plant material—not design. She still sees plant material as horticultural specimen not as units in design. Her primary concern is its condition.

Phase Two: Responds to design. "I like it" or "I don't like it." She responds to good or poor design but does not know to what design forces she is responding, so can not express herself in terms of design relationships or objectives.

Phase Three: Recognizes weaknesses. She can spot "What is wrong with it." It is always easier to point out what is poor or ill-conceived than to see what is good. She looks for deficiences and takes great delight in being able to point them out. She enlarges them beyond their significance in relation to the favorable design qualities.

Phase Four: "Corrects" or "improves" the design. She mentally or orally makes changes in the exhibitor's design that she feels would improve it and then judges the exhibitor's design in relation to her hypothetically improved version. Some judges find it difficult to refrain from reaching out and moving things around a bit.

Pointing out what the exhibitor might have done is not judging. There are dozens of changes that you or someone else might have made—in fact, there are no two people who, starting with the same material, would have developed the same design.

This does not deny that judges' comments are of value to the exhibitor. They may suggest a different approach to the use of material. In fact a workshop in which many possibilities with the same material are explored is most helpful. But what might have been done has no bearing on the exhibit to be judged.

Phase Five: Recognizes what the exhibitor has achieved. At this stage the judge evaluates the exhibitor's work in positive terms of what the exhibitor has achieved. She has now reached the status of a true judge.

Isolating the Structural Design. The black and white image above serves to isolate the structural design from the color design on the left.

Dynamic Balance. The dynamic linear movement in the design is sufficient to counteract the physical unbalance; thus rhythm and balance are co-ordinated to furnish dynamic balance.

THE JUDGING PROCEDURE

Everyone who visits a flower show is an unofficial judge. Have you ever followed two garden club members—from another club—around a flower show and considered their actions and remarks in regard to the arrangements?

They observe as they walk along looking at one arrangement after another. They allow each to register on their consciousnesses. During this period many arrangements are "eliminated" from consideration.

They react. "Wait a minute. Look at this one." (Comments that indicate their reactions.) What they observed has attracted them sufficiently to slow them down.

They evaluate. This may take but a fleeting moment or it may "tie up the line" as others following them may discover. They stop long enough to get the full impact that the arrangement has to offer. This is the crucial moment—the moment of evaluation.

They communicate their respective reactions. "Notice how!" or "Isn't this beautiful!" "Yes, but I like the one back there better." They may continue this discussion and each may decide on what she likes best. They may or may not take into consideration the class description, give their reasons for their choice, or reach a compromise.

Each selects her tricolor after making the round. One may go back and admire the arrangement that particularly appealed to her. Or she may even wait until after leaving the show to announce her decision. By this time most of the other arrangements have dropped out of her consciousness. "Do you remember that arrangement in the second row with the . . . " Her tricolor may stand out in her mind months later after the show is over.

The official judge proceeds generally thru this same procedure. She observes; she eliminates from consideration; she reacts favorably to others; she evaluates; she comes to a decision; she communicates her reaction or decision. But during this procedure she has responsibilities which materially affect her attitude toward the assignment she has accepted. She must give consideration to the factors which the unofficial judge could ignore.

1. She evaluates within the same limitations of the class wording which the exhibitor accepted when she made her entry.

2. She has a responsibility to justify her choice and must be able to do so. She may not need to justify her choice to the exhibitor, the flower show committee, the public or even to herself, but she must be prepared to do so to the other judges on her panel.

3. She may need to reconsider her own judgment in order to co-ordinate it with that of the other judges. Each judge must make an effort to see and feel what the other judges have experienced and to review her own first impression. She must not let herself be carried away by that first impression but must be willing to let more subtle meanings come through to her.

The judging procedure appears to be a simple process but the procedure is only the outward form of judging. The evaluation or judgment itself is an involved mental and emotional process.

THE JUDGE'S EVALUATION

What do we do when we judge? We must determine the answer to the following questions.

1. Has the exhibitor fulfilled the assignment she has accepted?

2. How *well* has she filled the assignment?

POINTS FOR CONFORMANCE

When an arranger enters an exhibit in a show she accepts the conditions imposed on all others exhibiting in the same class. These include the regulations imposed by the sponsoring body, the rules set out in the schedule, and the limitations of the class wording.

The regulations of the sponsoring body determine basically what may be entered in any of its shows. The purpose for which the organization is organized will largely determine what is eligible. This is true whether the organization is a garden club, a plant society, a county fair or an art museum.

The show schedule relates to the specific show at hand. It should and usually does limit or enlarge the scope of the show within the limits of the resources of the organization and the anticipated exhibitors. Such resources include time, talent, place, properties, etc.

Class limitations are set up to provide a common denominator for all arrangements to be considered at one time. This is out of fairness to the exhibitors. To judge a miniature against a formal table setting would be obviously unfair to both. Class limitations are not and should not be an attempt to stifle or suppress the ingenuity or creativeness of the arranger.

Most flower show committees provide a passing committee to pass on arrangements and to disqualify those not meeting the requirements or not within the limitations of the three categories set out above. The purpose is to screen arrangements for *specific* requirements such as use of fresh or dried plant material, size, etc. The passing committee does not pass on such *relative* aspects as suitability, style, interpretation and such other matters of judicial discretion which fall within the province of the judge. Thus some points should be provided in the scale of points for compliance. Has the exhibitor carried out her assignment? Do roses provide the dominant interest? Is the arrangement suitable for the outlined purpose? Is it the color plan called for in the schedule? Is the style free form? These and other considerations that deal with compliance can be grouped. The number of points may vary with the difficulty of the assignment.

All these considerations have no bearing on the quality of the design.

Conformance may be excellent, even though the floral design itself is poor. Conformance can be completely lacking, yet the design may be distinctive. The distinctive design that does not conform obviously should not rate as high as one that does.

POINTS FOR DESIGN

The bulk of the points in a scale should be allocated to design. How good is the design within the limitations of the class wording?

There are several ways to approach evaluation. The direct approach is to determine if the objectives of design, harmony, distinction and beauty, have been achieved.

The real test of good design is how rich or full an experience it gives those who view it.

The direct approach serves if the decision is clearcut and the judges are in accord.

Often the decision is not clearcut or the judges are not in accord. Then the comprehensive approach must be resorted to. This involves analysis of how the objectives have been achieved.

The following scale of points may be found useful. These may be adjusted according to the qualities that are emphasized in the class wording.

Conformance and Suitability 15

Structural Design (all principles) 40

Chromatic Design (all principles) 25

Distinction 20

Total 100

The black and white image on page 181 of the color photograph on the facing page serves to isolate the structural design from the whole. Although it is impossible to do this in actual judging, a conscious awareness of the existence of the two designs is essential to good evaluation.

"Structural Design," or the word "Design" used alone, implies the question: Are the elements of line, form, space, size, and form patterns organized according to design principles?

"Chromatic Design," "Color Design," or the word "color" used alone, implies the question: Are the elements of hue, value, texture, and color patterns organized according to design principles?

If a further breakdown of design qualities is deemed desirable, principles may be listed under each design and each evaluated separately. It should be borne in mind, however, that although both designs must be evaluated according to all principles (except the minor ones) proportion relates differently to each.

In structural design, proportion effects balance and rhythm, because it, too, is the result of placement. In chromatic design, proportion is a part of dominance, because here it is relative amount or magnitude.

DISTINCTION

Since the structural design and the chromatic design are judged separately, the co-ordination of the two designs is reflected in the points alloted to distinction. Distinction thus includes the harmony of these two designs, in addition to the many facets set out in a previous chapter.

The structural design and the chromatic design, whether good or poor, are inherent, but the quality of distinction must be created or achieved. So in scoring distinction it is desirable to use the positive approach: Do all respects add up to distinction? It would be unrealistic to start with a pre-conceived idea of what distinction should be and then take off points accordingly. The judge can however determine whether all the characteristics of an arrangement add up to distinction.

Originality or creativity are not set out as separate categories with their own allotment of points. Although a good judge keeps informed regarding all development in flower arranging, no judge can be familiar with every design ever created. A judge's capacity to judge originality or creativity is always limited by her own experience. She can never know definitely whether a design is an original or a copy; whether it was conceived in the mind of the exhibitor or whether the exhibitor saw it in a show the week before in another part of the state, or in another part of the country.

Thus the omission of the above categories is not intended to minimize their importance in design, but is an acceptance of the judges limitations to judge them. The judge can, however, consider these categories, in the light of her own experience along with all other considerations in arriving at distinction. In fact, it might be more correct to say that the judge will have difficulty ignoring them, in arriving at distinction.

INTERPRETATION OR EXPRESSION

If interpretation or expression is a part of class requirements, points should be allotted for them. The following scale may be found useful.

Conformance 10

Structural Design (all principles) 30

Chromatic Design (all principles) 15

Interpretation or Expression 25

Distinction 20

Total 100

An interpretative or expressive design should not only create a psychological impact but should include an emotional response. The communication between the arranger and the viewer is of a different nature and is subject to more variables. The arranger's past experience, her emotional response to her components, and her manner of organizing them, introduces three variables. The sum total of experience, emotional and otherwise, of the three judges adds three more variables.

JUDGING TABLES

It is desirable that a scale of points for judging tables should have some points allotted to the decorative unit alone, and other points to the relationship of the whole table, including the decorative unit. The decorative unit should be a harmonious unit in itself, and at the same time it should also be an integral part of the harmony of the table as a whole. As guests arrive at the table, or are seated, it should present a pleasing co-ordination of form and color of the arrangement, the table or cloth, and all appointments, At sit-down tables, as the meal gets underway, napkins leave the table, food is served up, and dinner plates give way to desert plates. At a buffet table, appointments leave the table, and partially filled serving dishes remain. Throughout all this to the last course at a sit-down meal, or for the last guest at a buffet table, the decorative unit should not be dependent on vanishing table appointments for its distinction or harmony. In fact, its independent attractiveness becomes even more important to its captive audience as the relationship of the other appointments disintegrates.

POSITIVE vs. NEGATIVE SCORING

In negative scoring we start with 100 points and *take off* for faults. In positive scoring we start with zero and *give points* for all that the exhibitor has achieved. The results should be the same, but unfortunately in actual practice they are not.

In reviewing the development of the judicial temperament, we note that the ability to discover weaknesses develops before the ability to analyze good design positively.

In negative scoring the exhibit loses points only for faults that the judge recognizes. The exhibit retains all others. The result is that the exhibit may be rated much higher than its good points would merit.

In positive scoring the exhibit is given points only for good design that the judge recognizes. The exhibit loses all others. The result is that the exhibit may be rated much lower than it merits. In this case the exhibitor is at the mercy of the imperfect judge.

Positive scoring — giving full credit for what the exhibitor has achieved — should be the ideal way to judge and should be a continuous goal. But perfection in judging, just as perfection in arranging, will long remain only a goal for us to strive for.

In the meantime, while we are striving for perfection, let us put greater emphasis on rewarding good design while recognizing faults in due perspective.

IN CONCLUSION

We have emerged from youth to maturity in Floral Design. We need no longer exist in the shadow of the other arts.

Every art form must be considered in terms of its contribution to the daily cultural needs of the greatest number of people. Flower arrangement meets that requirement — since the objectives of design are already partially present in flowers, flower arranging can enrich the lives of more people than any other art form.

It is true that flower arranging is a fleeting art — what is beautiful today, may be wilted tomorrow. But this is also true of many manifestations of beauty in nature. The glorious fall coloring of the woodlands may last but a few weeks; the spring burst of bloom on shrub or tree may last but a few days; the enchanting evening sunset may last but a few minutes. But tomorrow will be another enchanting sunset; next spring another burst of bloom; and next year another glorious autumn; and always there will be more and more beautiful arrangements to lift our spirits.

Glossary

ACCESSARY—An optional component. Anything other than plant material, container, background, or mechanics, subordinate in the design.

ACHROMATIC COLORS—Characterized by a complete lack of hue and chroma: pure black, white, and gray. Syn. with Neutral Colors.

ADVANCING HUES—Red and those hues in which red predominates. Syn. with Warm Hues.

AESTHETIC DESIGN—Design having attributes of harmony and beauty.

ANALOGOUS COLORS—Closely related colors. Generally, no less than three hues, no more than one pigment primary, and no more than one-third of the color wheel.

ANALOGOUS COLOR HARMONY—Analogous colors organized according to design principles.

ARRANGEMENT—See Flower Arrangement.

ASYMMETRICAL BALANCE—Balance without symmetry. Approximate equal visual weight composed of different elements on each side of an imaginary vertical axis.

BACKGROUND—A component of an arrangement. The surface against which an arrangement is seen; includes the areas in back of, underneath, above, and on either side of an arrangement.

BALANCE—A co-ordinating principle. Equilibrium between visual weights, attractions, or forces around an imaginary vertical axis.

BEAUTY—That intangible quality that evokes aesthetic pleasure and delight.

CHROMA—The third dimension of color. The degree of intensity or grayness, the strength or weakness, or the purity of a hue.

CHROMATIC COLORS—Colors having both hue and chroma. All colors other than the neutral colors.

CHROMATIC DESIGN—Design composed of the chromatic elements: hue and value, as modified by texture.

CLOSED FORM—A solid or completely enclosed hollow form; such as marigold, rosebud, apple, or pepper.

COLOR—A design element. The response of vision to reflected light rays.

COLOR ATTRIBUTES—see Color Dimensions.

COLOR CIRCLE—A circle composed of hues, in the same order as they appear in the solar spectrum, the number of hues depending on the color system used.

COLOR DIMENSIONS—Hue, value, chroma, Syn. with Color Attributes and Color Qualities.

COLOR FACTORS—Light, pigment, vision.

COLOR INTERVALS—The visual difference between hues on a hue circle, and between values and chromas on a color chart.

COLOR QUALITIES—See Color Dimensions.

COLOR SYSTEMS—An orderly classification of color by means of which color can be identified and described with precision.

COMPLEMENTARY COLORS—Hues directly opposite on the hue circle.

COMPLEMENTARY COLOR HARMONY—Complementary colors organized according to design principles.

COMPONENT—Physical material of which an arrangement is composed; such as plant material, container, feature, accessories, background.

CONTAINED FORMS—Forms having outlines that hold the eye within. All forms other than linear.

CONTAINER—A component of an arrangement. Any receptacle for cut plant material; includes bases, stands, mats, etc.

CONTEMPORARY STYLE—Any one of several styles of the present time.

CONTRAST—(noun) An inherent principle. A combination of opposite or unlike qualities, elements, or forces. (verb) Placing together unlike elements of the same class to emphasize differencs.

CONTRASTING COLORS—Combination of colors that are furthest apart as to hue, value, and/or chroma. Examples: red and green; light red and dark red; yellow and black.

CONVENTIONAL STYLE—According to guides, rules, codes, or frequently used design patterns.

CONVERGENCE—Lines coming together from several directions to one point. Opposite of Radiation.

COOL HUES—Blue and those hues in which blue predominates. Syn. with Receding Hues.

CO-ORDINATING PRINCIPLES—Principles that can be applied to co-ordinate the forces of the inherent relationships.

CREATIVE DESIGN—Free of rules, codes, or adherence to specific styles. May embody some characteristics of one or more styles.

DECORATIVE DESIGN—Design used to adorn a given place.

DESIGN—The organization of visual elements.

DESIGN ELEMENTS—The visual attributes of physical components, of which a design is composed.

DIRECTION—An inherent principle. Relative position of an element in regard to: 1. Its starting point. 2. Other elements.

DISTINCTION—Marked superiority in all respects.

DIVERSITY—A state of differing essentially. Differences existing between unlike classes.

DOMINANCE—A co-ordinating principle. The greater force exerted by one or more of the elements. Dominance implies the presence of Subordination.

DYNAMIC BALANCE—The equilibrium of the force of rhythm and the force of gravity.

EXPRESSIVE DESIGN—Design that communicates the arrangers own idea or mood.

FEATURE—An optional component. Anything other than the plant material, container, background, or mechanics, of dominant interest in the design.

FLORAL DESIGN—see Flower Arrangement.

FLOWER ARRANGEMENT—The organization of design elements, inherent in cut plant material and such other components as may be related thereto, with intent to induce an aesthetic appeal. Syn. with Arrangement, Floral Design, Design with Plant Material.

FORM—A design element. The outward contour of three-dimensional material. The term applies to the contour of the individual components as well as to the contour of the whole design.

FRAME—Border enclosing an arrangement. May be an actual frame, a Frame of Reference, or a visual frame.

FRAME OF REFERENCE—The border determined by the surrounding objects.

FREE-FORM—Free of conventional ideas, styles, and patterns, subject only to design principles.

FREE STANDING—To be viewed from all sides.

FRESH PLANT MATERIAL—The flower arranging medium. Any part severed from a living plant, with the quality of freshness unimpaired, and essentially unchanged in character. Includes flowers, branches, foliage, fruit, seedpods, etc.

FUNCTIONAL—Pertaining to implied or intended use or purpose.

GOLDEN MEAN—A ratio of 1 to 1.618; or roughly 1 to 1.6.

GRADATION—Variation at regular intervals in one direction or sequence.

HARMONY—The consistent, orderly, or pleasing arrangement of parts.

HIGH VISIBILITY HUES—Yellow and those hues in which yellow predominates.

HUE—A design element. The name of a color. The first dimension of color. The characteristic which distinguishes one spectrum color (as red) from another (as yellow-green, etc.)

INHERENT PRINCIPLES—Relationships that exist in every design.

INTERMEDIATE HUES—Hues between the primary and secondary hues. They bear the name of both adjacent hues, such as blue-green.

INTERPRETIVE DESIGN—Design that conveys a given idea, mood, theme, occasion, or atmosphere.

LINE—A design element.
1. A continuous unbroken visual path.
2. A sequence of similar forms that produce a visual path.

LINEAR FORM—A form in which length is the dominant dimension.

LOW VISIBILITY HUES—Violet and those hues in which violet predominates.

MECHANICS—Contrivances used to control the direction of material in the design.

MEDIUM—The material or means of expression used in any art. The medium in Flower Arranging is cut, fresh plant material.

MINIATURE—A design on a reduced scale.

MOBILE—A suspended design in which actual movement of its parts, or movement within the design, can be induced by air currents.

MODERN STYLE—Characterized by use of bold size, line, form, color, and/or texture, and by geometric pattern.

MONOCHROMATIC COLOR—A combination of values and/or chromas of a single hue.

MONOCHROMATIC COLOR HARMONY—
Monochromatic colors organized according to design principles.

MONTAGE—A floral design in which each component retains its identity and beauty while contributing its form and color to a harmonious while.

NATURALISTIC STYLE—Suggesting the natural growth habit of the plant material used.

NEUTRAL COLORS—Pure black, white, and gray. Characterized by a complete lack of hue and chroma. Syn. with Achromatic Colors.

OPEN FORM—A volumetric form; a form enclosing space. Examples: tulip, poppy, etc.

PATTERN—The silhouette created by a combination of lines, forms, colors, and the spaces between them.

PERIOD STYLE—that of a designated historical era.

PRIMARY COLORS—The colors from which, theoretically, all other colors are derived. The pigment primaries are red, yellow, blue.

PRINCIPLES OF DESIGN—Fundamental precepts based on natural forces that serve as guides to the aesthetic relationship of design elements.

PROPORTION—An inherent principle.
1. The relationship of the length, area, or volume of one part to another or of one part to the whole.
2. The relative magnitude of hue, value, chroma and/or color intervals.

RADIATION—Lines extending out in several directions from one central point. Opposite of Convergence.

RECEDING HUES—see Cool Hues.

RELEASING COLORS—Colors that do not stimulate attention: receding hues, hues of low visibility, dark values, grayed chromas.

RHYTHM—A co-ordinating principle. A dominant visual path.

SCALE—A minor principle.
1. Relative dimension of parts, without difference in proportion.
2. The size relationship of the component parts of an arrangement.

SCALE OF POINTS—The value of one quality compared to another, expressed in percentages.

SCENE—A miniature landscape.

SECONDARY HUES—Hues produced by the blending of two primary hues in equal parts. Pigment secondary hues are: orange, green, and violet.

SHADE—A dark value of a hue; a blend of pure hue and black.

SHAPE—A form predominantly two-dimensional.

SIZE—A design element. The dimensions of a line, shape, form, or space.

SPACE—A design element. The open areas within and immediately around the arrangement. The three-dimensional expanse within which an arrangement is organized.

SOLAR SPECTRUM—The spectrum produced by sunlight.

SPECTRUM—The colored image, produced by the refraction of light by a prism or other refraction device, in which the component light rays form a gradation in the order of their wave lengths.

STIMULATING COLORS—Colors to which the eye responds involuntarily: advancing and high visibility hues, light values, strong chromas.

STRUCTURAL DESIGN—Design composed of the structural elements: line, form, space, size.

STYLE—Characteristic manner of arranging.

SUBORDINATION—Subduing or making less forceful in relation to other elements in design. Implies the presence of Dominance.

SUBSTANCE—Internal structure; firmness; thickness.

SYMMETRICAL BALANCE—Approximate reverse repetition of elements on each side of a real or imaginary vertical axis.

SYMMETRY—Regular repetition of like or similar elements about a central point or axis.

TEXTURE—A design element. Surface structure.

TINT—A light value of a hue. A blend of pure hue and white.

TONE—A grayed hue.
1. A blend of pure hue and gray.
2. A blend of complementary hues.

TRADITIONAL—Handed down from the past; long established.

TRANSITION—Variation from one element or component through one or more intermediate ones to an unlike element or component.

VALUE—1. The second dimension of color: the lightness or darkness of a hue.
2. A design element: all variations of a single hue.

VARIATION—An inherent principle. Basic similarity with minor differences.

VOLUMETRIC—Three-dimensional space.

WARM HUES—Red and those hues in which red predominates. Syn. with Advancing Hues.

Index